T3-AJJ-942

EARLY SCHOOLING IN ASIA

|I|D|E|A| REPORTS ON SCHOOLING
John I. Goodlad, *General Editor and Director*

EARLY SCHOOLING IN ASIA

**Ruth Bettelheim and
Ruby Takanishi**

Introduction by
John I. Goodlad
Director, Research |I|D|E|A|
Dean, Graduate School of Education, UCLA
and
Samuel G. Sava
Executive Director |I|D|E|A|

A CHARLES F. KETTERING FOUNDATION PROGRAM

McGRAW-HILL BOOK COMPANY
New York   St. Louis   San Francisco   Dusseldörf   London
New Delhi   Singapore   Sydney   Toronto

124557

Copyright © 1976 by the Institute for Development of Educational Activities, Inc. All rights reserved. Printed in the United States of America. No part of this publication may be reproduced, stored in a retrieval system, or transmitted, in any form or by any means, electronic, mechanical, photocopying, recording, or otherwise, without the prior written permission of the publisher.

Library of Congress Cataloging in Publication Data

Bettelheim, Ruth.
  Early schooling in Asia.
  (Early schooling series) (|I|D|E|A| reports on schooling)
  "A Charles F. Kettering Foundation Program."
  Includes index.
  1. Education, Preschool—Asia. I. Takanishi, Ruby, joint author. II. Title. III. Series. IV. Series: Institute for Development of Educational Activities. |I|D|E|A| reports on schooling.
LB1140.2.B46 1976   372.21'095   76-25991
ISBN 0-07-005127-5

1 2 3 4 5 6 7 8 9 BPBP 7 5 4 3 2 1 0 9 8 7 6

|I|D|E|A| is the service mark for the Institute for Development of Educational Activities, Inc., an incorporated affiliate of the Charles F. Kettering Foundation.

|I|D|E|A| was established in 1965 to encourage constructive change in elementary and secondary schools. It serves as the primary operant for the Foundation's missions and programs in education.

As an institution committed to stimulating constructive changes for the benefit of mankind, the Kettering Foundation believes strongly in the potential of education to help bring about such changes.

Robert G. Chollar
President and
Chief Executive Officer
Charles F. Kettering Foundation

Acknowledgments for permission to use excerpts from copyrighted material include:

Myriam David and Irene Lezine, *Early Child Care in France*. Copyright 1975 by Myriam David and Irene Lezine. Used by permission of Gordon & Breach Publishing Co.

Lilian G. Katz, "Where Is Early Childhood Education Going?" Copyright 1973 by Lilian G. Katz. Used by permission of *Theory Into Practice*.

CONTENTS

124557

ACKNOWLEDGMENTS

The support of many individuals was invaluable to us in completing this book. John I. Goodlad, Research Director, |I|D|E|A|, provided overall support. The staff of |I|D|E|A| provided administrative and secretarial services and greatly facilitated the work. Judith Takata Hawkins served ably as research assistant in the often frustrating task of finding elusive documents and statistics on Asian preschools. John Hawkins, an Asian education scholar at the University of California, Los Angeles, reviewed the background sections on each of the countries. Individuals who assisted in the writing of each chapter are acknowledged in the chapter footnotes.

We owe a great deal of thanks to many other individuals. All the people who attended the Bangkok Conference on Preschool Education (listed in Appendix D) and many others helped us with background information, provided materials, arranged visits to schools, and prepared summaries about the early schooling scene in their own countries. Others reviewed the manuscript at various stages and made suggestions. These people are too numerous to list, but we do want to acknowledge their contribution.

Finally, Daniel John Flaming and Louis L. Knowles provided the intellectual and personal encouragement needed to sustain us in this endeavor.

Ruth Bettelheim
Ruby Takanishi

INTRODUCTION

The 1960s in the United States and many other countries were marked by proposals, often exuberantly presented and discussed, for extending formal education upward and downward and for enriching and broadening it horizontally. Some of the most optimistically received proposals pertained to the education of the young. Among these, Headstart probably enjoyed the most euphoric rhetoric.

The work of Piaget, which had been virtually ignored in this country except by a handful of scholars, became standard fare for students in psychology and education. Bloom's book,[1] stressing that approximately 50 percent of ultimate intellectual development takes place by the age of four, was identified as one of the most significant of the year, one likely to have a marked influence in years to come. Within a remarkably short period of time, scholarly thinking about the young child was being incorporated into far-reaching proposals for policy development. In California, serious attention was given to extending downward to four-year-olds opportunity to attend schools. The Educational Policies Commission mounted, with cost estimates, a similar proposal for the nation as a whole. And out of the Elementary and Secondary Education Act of 1965 came a much less ambitious but nonetheless bold proposal to create a multicentered National Laboratory in Early Childhood Education.

All of this now appears to be in some rather remote period in history. There are few remaining artifacts from the curricular effort to organize learning fare around the "structure of the disciplines" so that subjects would be taught in an intellectually honest form even to the

[1]Benjamin S. Bloom, *Stability and Change in Human Characteristics,* Wiley, New York, 1964.

very young.[2] The ambitious proposal of the president of the EPC faltered, along with the Council itself. Most of the resources intended for the Laboratory became artillery smoke over the hills of Vietnam. Ten years after the interest expressed during the 1960s, the California Legislature revised a new proposal for early childhood education so as to eliminate the provision of optional schooling for four-year-olds.

One could easily think that there has arisen some kind of conspiracy against the education of the young or that we have reverted to some earlier period of ignoring the existence of children in society, if it were not for the fact that this has been the fate of a host of proposals in many realms coming to the fore during the 1960s. Increasingly, we are realizing that a great many of the touted reforms and innovations were nonevents. They were widely discussed, conferences were held, plans were laid, but little implementation occurred.

One of the most difficult and significant lessons to be learned from the 1960s is that there was a great deal more smoke than fire. Some important conclusions about alternative programs can be derived *when there is clear evidence they were carefully installed and refined in practice.* But identifying the variables and attributing effects in natural experiments is a costly, difficult business. It is much easier simply to compare pupil effects as demonstrated by test scores without looking into the questions of extent and quality of implementation. As a consequence, we frequently and unwittingly conclude that something is impotent or ineffective when, in reality, it was never tried.

Many current proposals for educational improvement at all levels begin with the unexamined and often unquestioned assumption that innovations of the sixties are responsible for this or that shortcoming in the present. Whether or not the events occurred is not questioned; nor is whether the shortcoming exists. For many people, early schooling did not work and so it was abandoned. "Did not work" means it did not raise reading and math scores in the primary grades. The importance of raising scores, one among many possible functions of early childhood education, also is assumed, without regard for the sociopolitical reasons motivating much of the effort in the field. The danger in such thinking is that we hold up advancement or discredit ideas and proposals that deserve careful nourishment and rigorous testing.

Hardly anyone listened when Robert M. Hutchins quietly said, at the

---

[2]Jerome S. Bruner, *The Process of Education,* Harvard University Press, Cambridge, Mass., 1960.

height of Headstart, that the potential tragedy lay in concluding later, not that our strategies had been less than satisfactory but that the problems lie in the inability of children to learn. The evidence available today regarding children's learning capabilities is even more compelling than the evidence used in the 1960s to inform policy recommendations. Further, we have learned a little about how to put this knowledge to work for pedagogical purposes. Perhaps even more important, we have had considerable analysis of the change strategies employed for program implementation and, even though most of the inquiry has been at other levels, there are important implications for early childhood education. When the opportunity comes again—and it will—to provide more generously for the full educational development of the young, much will depend on whether we will be able to make productive use of these learnings. Certainly, the kinds of behaviors and talents being acquired and developed in the early years are no less important today than they were a decade or more ago when we talked so much about these matters.

Curiosity about the impact on practice of "the educational discovery of the young" in the 1960s was a motivating factor in the decision of the Institute for Development of Educational Activities, Inc. (|I|D|E|A|) to probe into the conduct of programs in early schooling. The work was placed under the coordination of John I. Goodlad. Earlier, he had studied curriculum reform of the time and observed the slippage from concept to implementation even in selected trial schools.[3] The problems of effecting change in schools appeared to be so important and troublesome that |I|D|E|A| launched a long-term inquiry into them in 1966. Major publications drawing from this Study of Educational Change and School Improvement have appeared as volumes in the |I|D|E|A| Reports on Schooling Series on Educational Change.[4]

---

[3]See John I. Goodlad, *School Curriculum Reform in the United States,* Fund for the Advancement of Education, New York, 1964; and John I. Goodlad, Renata von Stoephasius, and M. Frances Klein, *The Changing School Curriculum,* Fund for the Advancement of Education, New York, 1966.

[4]Carmen M. Culver and Gary J. Hoban (eds.), *The Power to Change: Issues for the Innovative Educator,* McGraw-Hill, New York, 1973; Richard C. Williams, Charles C. Wall, W. Michael Martin, and Arthur Berchin, *Effecting Organizational Renewal in Schools: A Social Systems Perspective,* McGraw-Hill, New York, 1973; David A. Shiman, Carmen M. Culver, and Ann Lieberman (eds.), *Teachers on Individualization: The Way We Do It,* McGraw-Hill, New York, 1974; Mary M. Bentzen and Associates, *Changing Schools: The Magic Feather Principle,* McGraw-Hill, New York, 1974; Kenneth A. Tye and Jerrold M. Novotney, *Schools in Transition: The Practitioner as Change Agent,* McGraw-Hill, New York, 1975; and John I. Goodlad, *The Dynamics of Educational Change: Toward Responsive Schools,* McGraw-Hill, New York, 1975.

This research suggests that models and strategies found to be useful for developing and disseminating new products and ideas are not equally useful for changing schools and classrooms. Such strategies appear to break down at school and classroom door. The Group on School Capacity for Problem Solving of the National Institute for Education has both recognized this in its Program Plan (1975) and funded several projects in light of this recognition. The |I|D|E|A| studies point to the need to foster decision-making capabilities in the individual school setting. Change is not something that moves inexorably and immaculately from conception of the big idea or governmental policy to the creation of new programs or renewal of old ones.

Since its inception in 1965, |I|D|E|A| has combined an interest in changes worth encouraging in schools, with inquiry into the process of change itself. In the late 1960s, it appeared that early schooling was an idea whose time had come. England has been a forerunner in the field and so it was thought useful to take a look there. If the British Infant Schools had something to say to us, presumably their nursery schools would, too. This proved not to be the case. The spirit of reform and enthusiasm had not touched, to any significant degree, the preschool level, according to Norma Feshbach who undertook the appraisal. There was, however, some awareness of a need for revitalization and a study designed to lay the groundwork was being considered at the time.

By the late 1960s, the work of Israeli scholars, such as Moshe and Sarah Smilansky, was becoming known in the United States. The problem of cultural disadvantage was uppermost in Israeli research and practice in early childhood education. The State had made a commitment to early schooling from the beginning (1948); the nature and extent of immigration created a special urgency. The problems of disadvantage in the United States were seen to have certain parallels in Israel. We asked Avima Lombard, who was familiar with developments in both countries, to report on program developments in Israel. The descriptions and analyses of both England and Israel were reported in a single volume.[5]

Our study of early schooling in the United States[6] took on a special interest when Goodlad, Klein, and Associates completed their look at

---

[5]Norma D. Feshbach, John I. Goodlad, and Avima Lombard, *Early Schooling in England and Israel*, McGraw-Hill, New York, 1973.
[6]John I. Goodlad, M. Frances Klein, Jerrold M. Novotney, and Associates, *Early Schooling in the United States*, McGraw-Hill, New York, 1973.

sixty-seven elementary schools in major population centers.[7] There was strong confirmation of that growing suspicion regarding the formidable gap between rhetoric and reality. But the kindergarten presented a somewhat different situation. More often than the primary grades, kindergartens presented a picture reasonably resembling the major recommendations of specialists in the field. Apparently, kindergartens have not yet rigidified into the sameness of climate and practice so often attributed to schools. Might not programs and practices in the nursery schools be even more encouraging?

This proved not to be the case. In our judgment, the nursery schools we visited were not, in general, as imaginative and exciting as the kindergartens observed in the earlier study. One explanatory thesis is that nursery schools are not closely tied to stimulation from outside sources, especially research and development. While we frequently decry the bureaucracy of the public school enterprise and attribute to it stultifying effects, the array of professional organizations, conferences, and inservice education activities in many different realms available through it no doubt helps considerably to update the knowledge and skills of teachers. Such opportunities are available only to the most affluent nursery schools and probably only when they make a deliberate effort to reach out for them. Teachers in most public schools receive considerable stimulation simply through a kind of osmosis. The problem common to all schools, however, as our research on change shows, is that of maintaining a continuous dynamic process of renewal which moves from discussion to decisions, actions, and evaluation.

The study of nursery school practices in selected Asian countries reported here is the final one in the |I|D|E|A| Early Schooling Series. More than the others, it was motivated almost entirely by simple curiosity about the relatively unknown and undescribed. Of all Asian countries, the educational system of Japan probably is best known to American educators. And, in recent years, we have come to realize that, as pointed out in Chapter 1, "Japan has one of the most extensive noncompulsory systems of early schooling in the world." Nonetheless we know very little about daily practices in these schools. We know even less about most other Asian countries.

We were interested, of course, in learning whether there was vigorous interest in the educational potentialities of the young and

[7]John I. Goodlad, M. Frances Klein, and Associates, *Behind the Classroom Door*, Charles A. Jones, Worthington, Ohio, 1970, revised and retitled, *Looking Behind the Classroom Door*, 1974.

whether these countries were busily endeavoring to translate this interest into vital programs. As in the United States, it appears that practices tend to reflect earlier thinking about appropriate nursery school activity for the young rather than the concepts and possibilities arising out of recent studies. In fact, at the conference of specialists in early childhood education which we arranged in Bangkok, there was general agreement among the Asian educators that the cognitive aspects of educational development ranked low in both the rhetoric of mission and the activities actually conducted. There was the admission, also, that gaining an early advantage in schooling was an interest of many parents, even though most justificatory language pertaining to attendance at nursery schools omits or speaks against preparation for school as an emphasis, while most of the programs provide for schoollike routines.

Even if we had gathered data on a great many schools, the ability to generalize across Asian countries and compare systems and practices there with those in England, Israel, and the United States would not readily emerge. Likewise, it would be dangerous to make recommendations for one country based on the practices of another. But, in spite of how often these caveats are articulated, we have a propensity for seeking to import highly touted programs with relatively little analysis of why they were developed elsewhere, why they worked, or why and how they might or might not be appropriate for our own educational settings.

Financial resources limited visits to only a few nursery schools in each country. Ruth Bettelheim conducted these visits diligently, taking advantage of every opportunity to discuss practices, points of view, and some of her own impressions with teachers and supervisors. She endeavored to discipline herself to record, not judge or interpret. This meant pushing aside, to the degree possible, some of the constructs guiding her own studies in psychoanalysis, psychology, and comparative education. Her purpose was to report faithfully what she perceived to be going on in classrooms, on playgrounds, or wherever else programs unfolded. Later, she had an opportunity to compare notes with another member of our staff, Jerrold M. Novotney, who visited nursery schools connected with the Catholic church in Asian countries.

The material for Chapters 1 and 9 and the background contextual sections of Chapters 2 through 8 were written by Ruby Takanishi. The nature of her previous and ongoing studies in early childhood development and education probably has resulted in a somewhat different orientation than would have been provided had Ruth Bettelheim written this part of the volume. The cross-national perspective she provides in the first chapter is an element not explicitly treated in the other two volumes of our Early Schooling Series. Her concluding chapter raises provocative questions for both early childhood education and comparative cross-cultural work in the field. We think that simply getting into print the information about early schooling practices in Asian countries is useful. But this contribution is vastly enhanced by the discussions of education in each country and the two general chapters mentioned above.

To both Ruth Bettelheim and Ruby Takanishi who worked independently on most of what follows, we express thanks and appreciation. We think their combined efforts have produced a readable, useful book. As with our other volumes on early schooling and educational change, this book has benefited in organization, style, and final wording from the high standards and continuous attention of our superb editor, Judith S. Golub.

Since we began the work reported here and in the books on early schooling in the United States and in England and Israel, the literature of the field has expanded considerably. This is particularly the case regarding the substance and methodology of cross-national research. Several major universities have strong programs in both research and the preparation of personnel at all levels.

With respect to policy and practice, we appear to be in a time of reflection and of taking stock. Presumably, we are sorting out and using what is of worth and casting aside the rest. Or are we in a period of regression and stagnation? The possibility that we are is nagging and disturbing.

The name of the game at the time of this writing appears to be power and who shall have it. Many of the matters being questioned have long gone unquestioned; opening them up for debate is overdue. Often, however, the scene denotes anarchy rather than the give-and-take of true debate. "Give me a piece of the action now and I'll worry about the substantive issues later," seems to describe much of what is bubbling in education today. The immediate concerns are more sociopolitical than the classic ones of who and what shall be taught.

There was a great deal wrong with the educational reform movement in the sixties. Most of all, the claims and expectations for schooling and education were overstated, sometimes outrageously so. Considerable disillusionment was an almost inevitable result. But there was hope, confidence, and excitement, too. And provocative ideas were at the heart of it all. Surely more of this is just ahead. In the field of early childhood education tomorrow, what will be the equivalent of the Bruner hypothesis regarding the young child's abilities and of the Bloom thesis regarding how much behavior is shaped during the early years? Will we be more successful in implementing the ideas that will shape tomorrow's policies? Perhaps what is the most encouraging is that the search for fundamental, potentially useful knowledge continues.

John I. Goodlad
Director of Research
and
Samuel G. Sava
Executive Director
|I|D|E|A|

EARLY SCHOOLING IN ASIA

CHAPTER 1

EARLY SCHOOLING IN CROSS-NATIONAL PERSPECTIVE: AN OVERVIEW OF THE FIELD

As Americans struggle with the uncertain legacy of the compensatory early education programs of the sixties and with the current challenge of providing comprehensive child development services for all children, they look to other countries for potential models and guidance. The impetus to learn what other countries are doing for their young children reflects a worldwide concern to improve the delivery and quality of supportive services to children and to their families. It is hoped that by sharing problems as well as solutions, each country can better evolve its own programs and policies to satisfy the problems posed by national and local conditions. For this reason, as well as for scholarly reasons, there has been tremendous activity in the cross-national examination of programs for children in the last decade.

This book on Asia is the final volume in the |I|D|E|A| Early Schooling Series, which was initiated by John I. Goodlad with the purpose of undertaking descriptive studies of programs below the compulsory education level in selected countries.[1] The first volume, *Early Schooling in the United States,* surveyed 201 schools in nine American cities and represents one of the few descriptive studies made of the American

NOTE: Parts of this chapter appeared in Ruby Takanishi, "Early Child Care and Education in Cross-National Perspective," *Review of Education,* vol. I, no. 4, November 1975, pp. 497–507.

preschool scene on a national scale. As a study of model as well as "average" preschools, the findings were sobering. Goodlad and his associates noted an incongruity between nursery schools as they exist in practice and the ideas and models which were being advocated by leading theorists.

In addition, a second volume focused on early schooling in England and Israel. American early schooling shares its roots and philosophical orientations with those of England. The interest in child welfare and education in American society has its historical origins in similar movements in England. Israel was studied because of its national policy of beginning education at four years of age and because of the challenges the country faces in assimilating large numbers of immigrants from diverse cultural backgrounds into Israeli society. Both these aspects of Israeli early schooling are of interest to American educators.

The first two volumes in the Early Schooling Series indicate that while all three countries have exemplary model programs, these programs reach only a small proportion of the age group. A theory-into-practice gap clearly emerges, and in this sense early schooling is similar to other levels of education. The reasons for this gap are more closely examined in the last chapter of this book.

This book provides the first overview of early schooling in Asia available in English and joins a growing literature placing early schooling in international perspective. Although in most of the countries discussed here early schooling is just emerging as a phase of the educational system, the history of program development in India and Japan has roughly paralleled that in America. In fact, Japan has one of the most extensive noncompulsory systems of early schooling in the world.

In addition to |I|D|E|A|'s work, other groups and individuals have also looked at early schooling from a cross-national perspective. Between 1969 and 1971, the International Study Group on Early Child Care, a coalition of specialists from twelve countries, began to exchange information on the partnership between society and the family in the care of young children. The work of this group has resulted in the International Monograph Series on Early Child Care, edited by Halbert B. Robinson and Nancy M. Robinson. At the Russell Sage Foundation, research is being conducted by Urie Bronfenbrenner, Sarane Spence Boocock, and others on child-care systems in Sweden, Israel, and the People's Republic of China.[2]

Less publicized work has also been going on. The Council of Europe has looked at problems, methods, and research in preschool education in European countries. A number of new journals, including *Assignment Children/Les Carnets de l'enfance* (UNICEF), *Early Child Development and Care,* and the *International Journal of Early Childhood Education,* focus exclusively on research on child care and education from cross-national perspectives.[3]

American interest in early child care and education in other countries partially reflects the search for solutions to our own problems of providing comprehensive services for children. However, while it is true that some countries have had a longer history of programs and also provide services for a larger proportion of the preschool-age population than does the United States, studies conducted thus far have revealed more shared problems than solutions. These include insufficient numbers of programs to meet existing needs, predominance of the private sector (in nonsocialist countries) in the care and education of children, segregation of children by socioeconomic background into kindergarten for the middle class and day care centers for the lower classes, controversies regarding the nature of goals of preschool programs, difficulties in providing a program which matches philosophy with goals, the lack of trained staff accompanied by low salaries and lack of status for individuals who work with children, concern regarding the transition from preschool to primary units, and the call for greater governmental involvement on the national level in the planning and financing of comprehensive services for children.

Thus it is difficult to determine to what extent cross-national studies have informed or can inform planning in the United States. In fact, one of the important things we have learned from existing studies is that the planning of programs for children must take into account the unique complex of factors—historical, sociocultural, political, economic, and educational—which influence a society's view of familial and nonfamilial agencies in early socialization. Findings from early schooling research in the Republic of China obviously cannot be applied directly in differing social, political, and economic conditions. However, understanding programs *within the context of a particular country* may provide us with perspectives from which we can more critically analyze efforts within American society.

EARLY SCHOOLING FROM A CROSS-NATIONAL PERSPECTIVE

Although cross-national study of early schooling is a fairly new field, a great deal of work has already been carried out by various international agencies, notably the World Organization for Early Childhood Education (Organisation Mondiale pour l'Education Prescolaire or OMEP). A number of international conferences have also been held to discuss the status of preprimary education, to make recommendations to national ministries of education, and to discuss experimentation within the field. The following overview is based on the discussions at these conferences as well as a review of existing cross-national studies.[4]

Conceptualizations of the Child and Family

Any attempt to discuss early schooling cross-nationally must take into account how the child is viewed and valued in a society.[5] Philippe Ariés, in documenting the emergence of the concept of childhood in Western Europe, noted that the idea or image of childhood prevailing in a society has a constitutional feedback to the social institutions of that society.[6] Anthropologists have pointed to the importance of cultural variables in determining how a society views children and their rights, obligations, and roles. However, it is clear from existing studies that we know relatively little about the image of the child as viewed by different cultural and national groups and even less about how these views are translated into everyday patterns of child rearing and the experience of the child.[7]

In her discussion of the family as educator, Hope Jensen Leichter makes several critical observations.[8] She notes that our difficulties in conceptualizing the child and his family are related to the limited views of the family which are reflected in the research on families and socialization processes. This research has focused mainly on the education of children by their parents in industrialized countries and tends to focus on mother-child interactions. Two general questions are relevant in this context: What do we mean when we use the term "family"? How do families really operate on a day-to-day, minute-by-minute basis which mediates their influence on the child's development? The answer to the first question is clear-cut. There are different definitions of the family and household unit in different settings. While the nuclear family is the focal unit in some societies, it is of little emotional importance in societies with extended kinship systems. However, our answer to the question becomes less certain as many societies, especially in urban areas, are undergoing rapid change.

The second question poses complex analytic issues. Family socialization, even within nuclear family systems, does not take place only within the mother-child dyad. As Leichter indicates, children influence and educate their parents, especially in immigrant groups and under conditions of rapid social and technological change. Siblings socialize each other in many different ways, depending on size and composition of the family group. Finally, the external social networks in which the family is embedded affect family processes. All these influence patterns are in turn characterized by changes in the development of the participants during the life cycle. Clearly, then, when one talks about the family in any society, there is a need to move from romanticism and polemics to a careful examination of families as they exist, develop, and change. In the context of questions of early schooling programs, this kind of examination could conceivably change many of our ideas of the functions and practices regarding care and education of young children.

It is interesting to note, however, that there appears to be a high degree of consensus regarding the view of the child and his family in international-level documents on early schooling. For example, the UNESCO Meeting of Experts on the Psychological Development of Children concluded that there are four overriding values in early childhood programs: (1) the primacy of the early years in the child's development, (2) the critical importance of the family in early socialization, (3) the development of the whole child, and (4) the child as an active learner.[9] These four components are reflected in almost all international documents regarding early schooling (see Appendixes A and B). The report of the UNESCO meeting discusses these components as follows:

Primacy of the Early Years "The period from birth to age six is characterized by the rapid physical and psychological development of the child. While this growth is continuous from birth to adulthood, the period of early childhood is especially important in establishing the basic pattern of development."[10]

Critical Importance of the Family "The family has an essential responsibility of guiding the development of young children. . . . The boundaries between family responsibility and state responsibility vary from country to country. . . . The participants affirmed that the actions of the state should seek to support the family rather than to take over its functions."[11] In noting the importance of the family, the participants moved from primary focus on the mother to include single parents, extended families, and communal life arrangements.

Development of the Whole Child "The appropriate goal of the educational process is the overall development of the child, cognitive, emotional, social, and physical. These aspects are closely related."[12]

Since this development proceeds in a unitary or holistic manner, every program for children should attend to the whole child.

The Child as Active Learner   "Children should be actively involved in the learning process. They are assiduous explorers and exploiters of the physical and social worlds in which they grow up, constantly seeking new challenges and new solutions to the problems they encounter.[13]

Although there is agreement regarding these values, there is great variation among countries and within any country between expressed goals and values and actual implementation. Although there is firm agreement regarding the importance of the early childhood years, the development and expansion of programs for children has been relatively slow. Preschools are typically left to local authorities or to private enterprise and individuals. The continents of Asia (except for Japan and the People's Republic of China), Latin America (except for Cuba), and Africa are still pioneering programs. Within Europe, the western and northern countries (except for Belgium, the Netherlands, and France) lag behind those of Eastern Europe. Children in rural areas and central city areas often do not have access to preschool facilities.[14]

Although family and state responsibility for children varies with the social and political orientations of individual countries, all the international documents produced by international agencies note that the role of the preschool is to support and complement the role of the mother and family. In no way, even in socialist countries, is it intended that the home be supplanted by the preschool. However, it is generally agreed that preschools can compensate for inadequacies in the home and family situation which might interfere with the child's development and readiness for the primary school experience. Parent education and involvement has been considered an ideal, but this component has proved difficult to implement in practice.

In actual programs, the "whole child" philosophy common to the American early education movement is reflected worldwide. The development of the child is conceived as orderly, sequential, and continuous, and since this development proceeds in a holistic manner, the goals of programs should focus on the whole child—his physical, cognitive, social, and emotional development. When reading the literature of programs in individual countries, one is struck by the similarities in the descriptions of daily schedules and program goals and content. Children in early schooling programs draw, paint, dance, sing, and learn about nature and about cooperative life in group situations. Play is considered to be central to the curriculum, which ideally stresses discovery and independence. The imperative for teacher behavior is to be warm and supportive and to facilitate learning for the active and curious child. To some extent, this similarity is due to the fact that current practice worldwide has been influenced by Comenius, Pestalozzi, Froebel, Montessori, and native educators who derived their practices from these individuals. However, we have almost no cross-national data based on systematic observation of *actual* teacher-child, child-child, and child-environment interaction in ongoing programs. It is possible that such observation may reveal subtle but significant differences in curriculum, practice, and outcomes which are not evident from present descriptions and documents about goals. Critical to cross-national studies is the question of whether and how the experience of early schooling differs for children in different countries. The question of cultural influences on early schooling practice has not yet been addressed.

Consistent with the orientation toward the total development of the child, the ideal expressed in all international documents is delivery of comprehensive and integrated services to children and their families. However, in many countries, there is segregation in both type and availability of preschool programs. Kindergartens or programs with an educational bent are typically private, located in urban areas, and available to middle- and upper-class families. Nurseries or day care centers are supported by public welfare agencies and typically provide care for children of working mothers or for families in designated categories of social problems. Typically, the focus in these programs is on the provision of health services and care of physical needs. There is concern in some countries that this dual system of child care and education denies equal opportunity and, therefore, should be integrated under one agency, usually the ministry of education.*

Because of the segregation in the provision of these services, there is often a multiplicity of uncoordinated agencies and organizations which administer programs for children and their families. Communication and

---

*The usual distinction between kindergartens and day nurseries in terms of the "educational" function of the former is not clear-cut. Some kindergartens function as custodial units, while some day nurseries may provide an educational program (for example, in Japan). However, Lawrence Cremin has expanded the definition of education to include all agencies involved in the transmission of "knowledge, values, attitudes, skills, and sensibilities." Education takes place not only in schools but in churches, community settings, and peer groups and through the media (Lawrence A. Cremin, "Notes Toward a Theory of Education," *Notes on Education*, no. 1, pp. 4–5, Institute of Philosophy and Politics of Education, Teachers College, Columbia University, New York, June 1973). In line with Cremin's definition, a child receives education whether she is in a day care center or in a kindergarten.

planning among these organizations are often lacking, reflecting the lack of a comprehensive social policy regarding children and their families.

What the cross-national literature indicates, then, is that there is a gap between the expressed goals and conceptualizations of the child and actual practice. What is seriously lacking in the discussions is the fact that the provision of services and programs for children and families is a political issue which involves social values and philosophies, economic constraints, and, to some extent, research evidence. Program development is a dynamic process in which overt and hidden conflicts over societal goals and the role of the family come to a head. We must take account of ideologies regarding the child and the family when attempting to understand the meaning and the provision of early child care and education. Hence, any study of early schooling must seriously confront the politics and ideology surrounding its provision. With regard to this point, it is useful to examine the expressed functions of early schooling.

Functions of Preschools

The expressed functions of early schooling vary from one country to another. However, there are some notable similarities in how preschools are perceived in relation to the social, cultural, political, and economic needs of the society.

Preschools are believed to serve compensatory goals of equalizing social and educational opportunity for children. In most nonsocialist countries, controversies focus on the role of the state in the provision of preprimary education. These controversies are typically centered on the role of the family—or more precisely the mother—in early upbringing and on the costs of providing for this level of education given national priorities for providing compulsory and adult education. However, it is generally agreed that preschool education should be provided by the state for four special categories of children. The first category includes children from socioculturally or economically disadvantaged families. In European countries, these children may be dependents of foreign workers who remain in the country for various lengths of time. In many cases, those children need to be assisted in the acquisition of a second language before entering primary school. In the second category are children with physical or mental handicaps due to congenital or acquired defects. The third category contains children of working mothers, and the fourth children from families with special problems such as abuse, physical or mental illness, and single parents. These categories reflect the compensatory and preventive roles of the preschool which were explicit in its early origin as a place to protect and socialize children of the lower classes. The recent American experience with the compensatory early education programs of the sixties is seen as a model for social reform by many countries.

Throughout the world, the preschool is seen as having the function of preparing children for schooling in terms of appropriate expectations, values, behaviors, and, in some cases, basic academic skills. The curriculum traditionally has been informal with emphasis on learning through play and the development of creativity, independence, healthy self-concept, self-reliance, and cooperative group behavior. The subject areas tend to include music, art, nature study, and physical and motor activities. Although there have recently been a number of experimental programs, most children experience a program approximating the teachings of one or more of the four founders of the field—Froebel, Comenius, Pestalozzi, and Montessori.

Preschools are also identified with the preparation of children for social, economic, and political roles in a society. After periods of revolution, a great deal of attention is paid to the establishment of preschools as a means of unifying the new society and its ideals. For example, in Cuba, a central goal for the formation of the national network of child-care centers is the development of "the new Cuban man."[15] Political socialization and ideological orientation are also important functions of Soviet and Hungarian preschools. In a developing country such as India, the preschool is viewed as being influential in the creation of the new "technological man" who can make the transition from a primarily agrarian culture to one in which technological understanding is critical for national development.

Transition between Preschool and Primary Units

Another international concern is the relationship of preschools to primary-level education. If the number of children who experience some form of early schooling continues to increase, important questions must be raised as to needed continuity and changes in curriculum and in the roles of teachers and children in these two units. Except for a small number of experimental programs, these two units are separate, and there is limited interaction between them in all countries. One common issue focuses on the role of academic training in preprimary settings: Is the role of the school to prepare the child for successful primary school experience? Should a more structured curriculum be organized to improve the child's readiness for primary-level schooling? A related question is whether preschool units should be attached to primary schools, presumably to ensure continuity. Participants at the 1974 UNESCO conference noted that it was important to provide transitions "between the more-or-less distinct and largely arbitrary components of the nurturing process which [violate] the principle of continuity of development. . . ."[16] While the consensus appears to be that each unit should remain separate in terms of its buildings, staff, and equipment, many countries are nevertheless experimenting with the integration of the two units to ensure educational continuity.

In a sense, early education and child care must be directed toward facilitating the development of children who will be able to cope with multiple-role demands in a changing society. However, very little thought appears to be directed toward the effect of the early schooling experience in either facilitating or hindering the child's later development and adaptability in the wider world.

The emergence of concern regarding early schooling reflects what Lawrence Cremin refers to as changes in the "configurations of education."[17] The relationships among educational institutions in the society, including the family, at a given time and place shift with changes in social conditions so that the question of allocation of educational functions is likely to enter the public policy realm. In many countries, the increased participation of mothers of preschool children in the labor force and the disappearance of the extended family network are and will continue to be important factors influencing the expansion of early schooling.

Meanwhile, however, preschool education continues in most countries to be an educational orphan, except in programs for special categories of children. This situation reflects a lack of resources, but even more importantly, the provision of services to children is an integral part of questions of values and ideologies regarding the child, his family, and his culture. Two major factors appear to contribute to the slow rate of growth of early schooling programs. First, preschool education is often seen as a threat to the family and to its role in the socialization of children. Governments take little responsibility for children, except in cases where the family is not able to fulfill or has abdicated its responsibilities. Second, education is seen increasingly as serving an investment function, especially in developing countries, for national and economic productivity. Within this context, the payoff from the investment of resources in preschool education is not yet clear.

EARLY SCHOOLING IN ASIA

One of the neglected areas in cross-national studies in early schooling, with the possible exception of the People's Republic of China, has been the countries of Asia. Although in many of these countries early education and child-care programs reach only a small proportion of the population, the numbers reached are still impressive. Programs in India, for example, reach only 2 percent of the preschool-age population in the country, but the number of children served (more than 2 million in 1969)[18] exceeds the population of many small countries. In contrast, Japan has one of the highest proportions of children enrolled in preschool programs below the age of compulsory schooling, second to that of France.[19] This study of early schooling in seven Asian countries— Hong Kong, India, Japan, the Republic of Korea, Malaysia, the Philippines, and Thailand—is intended to fill a gap in the developing field of cross-national studies of programs for young children.

This book must be considered to be a survey of early schooling in selected Asian countries during the period of the late sixties and early seventies. Our purpose is to indicate what provisions for young children are available within each of the countries, not to attempt to compare them. Each country must be considered a separate case study. We do not claim to provide a complete view of preschools in any one country, since there is much variation in facilities, philosophy, curriculum and methods, and teachers, as well as regional differences within the same country. Also, in countries such as Japan and India with large numbers of children in preschool programs, an intensive study of their systems would require several books. It is hoped that the information presented in this survey will provide a basis for such intensive studies in the future.

A second reason for considering this book a survey is that the field of cross-national inquiry in early child care and education is a developing one and thus can be characterized as being largely at a descriptive phase.[20] Descriptive studies are important in providing a starting point, but it must be remembered that there are many pitfalls in descriptive inquiry because of the variety of conceptual and methodological approaches in the field. For example, a country's conceptualization of the family and the child is a critical factor in determining the nature and extent of the provision of preschool services.[21] However, as discussed previously, this conceptualization has proved very difficult to articulate.

In Asian countries, there is a paucity of research on family socialization patterns. Studies conducted by both Western and indigenous researchers have been heavily influenced by a tradition of socialization research which reflects a psychoanalytic orientation. The work of Sears, Maccoby, and Levin, which involved an attempt to test aspects of psychoanalytic theory using learning theory concepts,[22] is a model which is often used to guide research. Hence, researchers focus on child rearing in the areas of aggression, moral values, and traits related to achievement/competition and dependence/independence, areas which may be imbued with different meaning and functional value within the specific culture under study.

An additional problem is that within some of the Asian countries covered in this book, the heterogeneous composition of the population defies a simple or general description of the child and his family. This is especially true in the Philippines and in India, where many ethnic and tribal groups with different traditions and languages compose the national population. Hence, it was beyond the scope of this book to deal with the critical issues of family socialization practices and conceptualization of the child, which are integral to understanding a country's early schooling system.

In this context, we find Robert LeVine's speculative analysis of cross-cultural parental goals relevant.[23] On the basis of his fieldwork in a number of different cultures, LeVine suggests that child-rearing practices represent parental adaptation to environmental conditions which threaten the health and welfare of young children rather than a reflection of moral values or repressed motives. His perspective indicates that we must be cautious in describing and interpreting behaviors of individuals in different cultures without having an adequate understanding of the environmental pressures and constraints on the culture.

Our own observations suggest the utility of LeVine's work in future descriptive inquiries. In Hong Kong, for example, children in some preschools appear to be highly regimented. They are expected to stand in line, march in line, and respond in unison to the teacher. LeVine's hypothesis suggests that this regimentation may reflect environmental conditions, such as the small physical facilities of the classrooms, which are often located in large housing projects, and the large numbers of children in relation to the number of adult care givers, rather than a cultural orientation toward strict obedience. The classroom experience may be directed toward developing a pattern of behavior which is conducive to life in a densely populated urban society.

An additional consideration suggested by LeVine's work is the question of the importance of parental goals in determining early schooling practices. As will be seen in later chapters, in many of the Asian countries, preschool education is viewed as the first step in a highly competitive educational system which is an essential vehicle for social and economic mobility. In these countries, there is great pressure for the preschools to teach basic skills and orientations necessary for educational success in succeeding levels. This pressure is often in conflict with the traditional beliefs of early educators that stress the importance of providing a situation for informal learning in which play is the basis for cognitive, social, and emotional development. In reviewing early schooling programs, we must ask ourselves how the experience provided for the child reflects parent's goals in sending their children to preschools.

These are, of course, untested yet intriguing lines for future inquiry, but they also illustrate the caution with which descriptive work and interpretation must be approached and the conceptual task which lies before workers in the field. Future directions for conceptual and research endeavors in early schooling cross-nationally will be offered in the final chapter of this book.

EDUCATIONAL SYSTEMS IN ASIA: A BRIEF HISTORY

It is impossible within the scope of this book to provide a detailed historical, social, or economic analysis of the seven countries studied. Although basic demographic data are provided in Appendix C, we feel it is necessary to provide some background information on the historical context in which the educational systems of these countries have developed. Detailed information on each country's educational history and school system can be found in the chapter on that country.

In all the countries in this study, the pre-Western period was characterized by a form of education which was often closely associated with religious institutions. In many Buddhist countries, education in temples was available for children of commoners. In countries under Chinese influence during this period (Hong Kong and Korea), pre-Western education was secular, characterized by Confucian learning.

From the 17th to the 19th century, Western influence was felt both in independent nations and colonial nations. In the colonial countries

(Hong Kong, India, present-day Malaysia, and the Philippines) education developed in the absence of a policy of the ruling powers, and thus it was left to missionary groups and philanthropic efforts. The missionaries did much to support popular education and the development of native languages. Their work has had an enduring impact on Asian schooling, especially on the provision of early schooling.

Following the laissez faire period, the colonial governments began to play a more prominent role in the development of educational programs. This period of influence has had long-term consequences for the educational systems of some Asian countries in terms of the problems which they continue to face today.[24] First, the educational model of the colonialists was an elite one in which a limited number of individuals, typically from the upper classes, were trained to fill roles in the colonial administrative bureaucracies. Hence, primary education for the general population was neglected while secondary and higher education institutions were developed for a small number of students. Two exceptions were Japan and the Philippines. When making a transition from a feudal society to a modern state, Japan placed a priority on the development of primary education for the general population. In the Philippines during the American colonial period, the Americans established free public elementary schools for the population.

Another consequence of colonial influence was that the educational system was urban not only in location but also in orientation, curricula, and method. The urban bias tends to be a continuing problem in India, for example, where 80 percent of the population is located in rural areas. Similar problems are currently being faced in the Philippines, Malaysia, and Thailand. These countries have consequently begun to evolve strategies to educate rural populations and to meet rural conditions.

An enduring consequence of the British colonial influence is the examination system, which in some countries still determines passage through various educational levels. The examinations were identical to those administered in British schools, and they dominated the curriculum and teaching methods in countries which were culturally different. The persistence and pervasiveness of the examination system have had important implications when countries have tried to use their educational systems to promote national identity and cohesion.

During the post-World War II period, which was accompanied by the achievement of national independence in many colonial countries, large-scale educational reform began, most noticeably in the expansion of primary education. It is critical to note, however, that much quantitative expansion took place within existing structures and was often not related to reforms in the organization and objectives of education. During this period, the national language began to be used in instruction as a means of creating national unity as, for example, in Malaysia. Curriculum reform centered on adapting education to complement local traditions and conditions. The achievement of a universal system for primary education continues to be an important educational goal in many of the countries, and, as a consequence, the development of early education programs has been hindered.

We have sketched here the general educational context of the countries studied. There are great variations among them as to the extent of their economic and educational development. Even within a single country, there are variations based on urban-rural differences and on the social and cultural backgrounds of the students. These variations are a worldwide phenomenon.

THE STUDY

For the purposes of this study, early schooling is defined as the care and education of children below the legal age of admission to the first year of compulsory primary education. In most countries studied, the majority of the children enrolled in preschools are between the ages of four and six. While there is preschool provision in some of the countries for children below three years of age, this age group accounts for a very tiny percentage of the total preschool enrollment in each country studied except Japan, where day nurseries serve children from birth to six years. For this reason, only programs designed for children between the ages of three and six were observed.

Definitional confusion is a common problem in cross-national studies of early schooling. In most of the Asian countries the term "kindergarten" is used to describe what Americans call both nursery schools and kindergartens. Kindergartens are typically half-day programs for children from three to six years of age. A majority of Asian kindergartens are private, and there is only a small number of public or demonstration kindergartens. In all cases, the kindergarten, which began appearing in the late nineteenth century, was an import from Western countries. The terms "nursery school" and "day nursery" refer to day care programs, typically regulated by welfare officials, which often serve children below three years as well as the age range served by the

kindergartens. Day nurseries are all-day programs for low-income families, children of working mothers, and families with special problems.
The growth of day nurseries increased during the post–World War II
period, accompanied by and seemingly related to industrial development and increased participation of mothers of young children in the
labor force.

Table 1.1 presents an overview of early schooling in selected Asian
countries based on the 1971 UNESCO *Statistical Yearbook*. The table
summarizes information on preschool age limits, the age of compulsory
schooling, the number of schools and teachers, the enrollment of the
preschools, and finally the proportion of the age group enrolled at first-
level education. Since preschool education is largely part of the private
sector, statistical information on this level is difficult to obtain. Hence,
the statistics in Table 1.1 must be viewed as minimum estimates. Where
possible, the UNESCO office excluded data on nurseries.

Procedures and Data Sources

Various sources of information were used in developing the descriptions
of preschools in seven Asian countries.[25] First, coauthor Ruth Bettelheim
visited, on the average, six preschools in each country during the period
from September 1969 to January 1970. Countries were selected on two
bases: the development of interest in preschool education in the country
and available contacts with individuals in the field. In each of the
schools visited, both children and teachers were observed from the time
they arrived at the beginning of the school day until the time they left.
The behavior of the head teacher of a single class was recorded during
this visit. These running record observations focused on describing
teaching methods, curriculum, equipment, and facilities. The observations, together with information derived from other sources described
below, provided the material for the descriptions of the school day
which follow the presentation of background information on each
country.

The presence of an observer, particularly a foreign observer, always
has an impact on the classroom behavior of both teachers and children.
In general, when outside observers visit a school, teachers and children
try to be on their best behavior. Sometimes attempts in this direction fail,
especially with very young children, but all people tend to put their best
foot forward for guests. Bettelheim went to each school as an invited
guest. The school was informed of her visit approximately one day to

TABLE 1.1 EARLY SCHOOLING IN SELECTED ASIAN COUNTRIES*

Country	Preschool Age Limits	Age of Compulsory Schooling	Year	Schools	Teachers	Enrollment†	Enrollment Ratio at First Level‡
China, Republic of	4-6					91,984	99.9
Hong Kong	3-5		(1969)	840	3,352	134,858	99.9
India	3-6	6-14	(1965)		215,220	9,186,000	56.0
Indonesia	4-7	8-14	(1969)		10,621	343,466	70.0
Japan	3-5	6-15	(1969)	10,418	69,095	1,551,017	99.9
Korea, Republic of	4-6	6-12	(1970)	484	1,660	22,271	99.9
Laos	4-6	6-9	(1969)	13	17	528	47.0
Malaysia§							
Sabah	4-6	6-13	(1968)	20	51	1,531	99.9
Sarawak	4-6	6-12	(1970)	68	151	4,907	87.0
West Malaysia	4-6		(1969)	332	736	21,194	89.0
Mongolia	3-8	8-15	(1970)			32,000	
Philippines	3-7	7-13	(1967)	373	840	38,975	99.0
Thailand	4-6	7-14	(1968)			102,370	80.0
Vietnam, Republic of	4-6	6-11	(1969)		1,195	73,281	90.0

*Figures are for children aged three through age of compulsory schooling. UNESCO *Statistical Yearbook*, 1971.
†Enrollment figures should be considered as minimum since complete data are not available in all cases.
‡Ratios of 99.9 indicate the approximate achievement of universal education at the first level. (Actual ratios in the UNESCO *Statistical Yearbook* [1971] exceeded 100 when age distribution of pupils at the first level spread over official school ages for the level.)
§Separate statistics are given for the three Malaysian states because they differ so widely.

one week in advance. Some made obvious efforts to impress; others did not. The observations may tend to be biased in the direction of what the teachers consider to be ideal examples of good programs in preschools, but observation of what is considered to be ideal or as close to it as possible helps to define more precisely the nature of a school's goals or objectives. It gives us an idea of what is aimed for and what is valued. Since education is a vehicle for the transmission of culture, the distortion caused by the presence of an observer, while real, is no hindrance to understanding cultural differences in educational practices.

In each country, several different types of schools were visited. The schools were selected by persons directly involved in the field of preschool education in each nation, such as preschool teacher trainers, directors of research institutes, researchers in the field, staff members of the preschool sections of the ministry of education, presidents of preschool education associations, and preschool directors. All were asked to select preschools representative of preprimary educational practice in their countries. In Japan, the Republic of Korea, Malaysia, and the Philippines, schools considered exemplary were selected. In Hong Kong, India, and Thailand, schools representative of a very wide range of educational provision were chosen. The sample of schools observed in each country is presented in Table 1.2.

TABLE 1.2   SAMPLE OF ASIAN SCHOOLS VISITED BY BETTELHEIM

Country	Number of Schools			Sponsorship		Total Enrollment (all schools observed)
	Total	Urban*	Rural	Private	Public	
Japan	5	4	1	3	2	1,169
Korea, Republic of	3	3	0	3	0	340
Hong Kong	5	5	0	4	1	961
Malaysia	5	4	1	5	0	1,138
Philippines	4	4	0	2	2	1,132
Thailand	6	4	2	2	4	838
India	6	6	0	3	3	795
Total all countries	34	30	4	22	12	6,373

*Cities with populations greater than 100,000.

Another important source of information for the descriptions of the school day was the observations made in Roman Catholic preschools of these countries by Jerrold M. Novotney, who has specialized in the study of church-related education. These observations were made in schools different from those visited by Bettelheim. Rather than spending an entire academic day in one school, Novotney spent parts of each day in different schools. In this way, he was able to observe an average of four schools in each of the countries and hold interviews with teachers and headmasters.

An equally important source of information was a conference of preschool experts held in Bangkok, Thailand, from December 3 to 5, 1969. This conference was convened especially for the purpose of amplifying and clarifying the impressions of the |I|D|E|A| research team. Outstanding experts and leaders in the field of early schooling from each country presented papers describing various aspects of preschool education. The participants are listed in Appendix D. Additionally, these individuals gave a detailed description of classroom practices in their countries. The researchers also requested information or correction of their own observations. The information gathered from these Asian preschool experts was incorporated into the individual chapters. We are deeply grateful for their assistance. However, we remain responsible for any inaccuracies and shortcomings in the descriptions.

In addition, in order to update the information gathered through observations and at the conference, the existing literature in the field was studied. Statistical data and published reports in English and the national languages were reviewed. We wrote to researchers, officials, and practitioners in the countries, requesting information on various aspects of early schooling. Relevant documents were translated from the national language.

In summary, the information sources which provided the basis of our study of early schooling in Asia were English and native language reports and documents on early schooling; questionnaires and interviews conducted with a small sample of government officials, principals, teachers, and researchers in each country; a limited number of observations in the schools in the countries; and feedback by Asian early schooling educators on these observations.

Organization of Each Chapter

In providing a description of early schooling in the seven Asian countries, a primary concern was to present an overview of the current state of early schooling in each country. We also attempted to remain sensitive to the questions which Asian countries and their educators might have regarding problems of early schooling. As mentioned earlier, the nature and provision of early schooling must be viewed in the context of the educational system of each country. Hence, each chapter typically begins with a brief educational history and outline of the educational system of the country. Then the focus is on the preschool programs in terms of their historical and social development, organization and administration, and statistics. A description of curricula, classroom practices, activities, and equipment for early schooling programs is presented. Observations of the school day in programs which were visited by Bettelheim are included for each country. Because of the difficulty of obtaining comparable information for each country, each chapter is organized somewhat differently, but an attempt was made to follow the same outline whenever possible.

This book has three general purposes within the field of cross-national studies of early schooling. First, this chapter has provided an overview of the field in terms of the goals and problem areas in studies of early schooling. The second and primary purpose of the book is to provide descriptive information on the state of early schooling in selected Asian countries (Chapters 2–8). It is hoped that this information will provide a basis for communication among Asian countries regarding early schooling and will provide background information for Americans who have an interest in the Asian region. The concluding chapter stresses the need for conceptual as well as methodological tools for future international studies on schooling. As we learn more about programs in individual countries, the realization of the enormous task we have before us to understand the development, as well as the present functioning, of these programs and their relationship to the development of children and the role of the family in early socialization will become even more apparent.

NOTES

1   John I. Goodlad, M. Frances Klein, Jerrold M. Novotney, and Associates, *Early Schooling in the United States,* McGraw-Hill, New York, 1973; Norma D. Feshbach, John I. Goodlad, and Avima Lombard, *Early Schooling in England and Israel,* McGraw-Hill, New York, 1973.

2   See U. Bronfenbrenner, "Eleven Blind Americans and the Chinese

Child," *Newsletter of the Society for Research on Child Development,* Fall 1974.

3 A list of informational sources on cross-national perspectives on child care and early education is available in Sarah Moskovitz, "Cross-Cultural Early Education and Day Care: A Bibliography," ERIC-Early Childhood Education Publication, Catalog Number 129, Urbana, 1975.

4 Conference proceedings reviewed included the International Bureau of Education and UNESCO, *Organization of Pre-Primary Education,* XXIVth International Conference on Public Education, Geneva, 1961 (Appendix A contains the recommendations of this conference); International Bureau of Education and UNESCO, *Initiatives in Education: A World Profile for 1971–1972,* Paris and Geneva, 1972; Tessa Blackstone, *Preschool Education in Europe,* Council of Europe, Strasbourg, France, 1970 (ED 047 779); UNESCO, *Final Report of Meeting of Experts on the Psychological Development of Children and Implications for the Educational Process,* Champaign-Urbana, Ill., March 4–9, 1974 (mimeographed); and Council of Europe, *Recommendations of the Venice Symposium on Preschool Education,* October 1971 (see Appendix B).

5 The books in the International Monograph Series on Early Child Care (Halbert B. Robinson and Nancy M. Robinson, eds.) deal with national conceptualizations of children and families. The degree of success varies by the individual monograph. However, as noted in Chapter 9, there are difficult conceptual and methodological issues involved in this area of inquiry.

6 Philippe Ariés, *Centuries of Childhood,* Vintage, New York, 1962.

7 International Monograph Series on Early Child Care. See also Robert A. LeVine, "Parental Goals: A Cross-Cultural View," *Teachers College Record,* vol. 76, pp. 226–239, December 1974.

8 Hope Jensen Leichter, "Some Perspectives on the Family as Educator," *Teachers College Record,* vol. 76, pp. 175–217, December 1974.

9 UNESCO, Final Report, op. cit.

10 Ibid., p. 10.

11 Ibid., p. 11.

12 Ibid., p. 10.

13 Ibid.

14 Blackstone, op. cit.

15 Marvin Leiner, *Children Are the Revolution,* Viking, New York, 1974.

16 UNESCO, Final Report, op. cit.

17 Lawrence A. Cremin, "Notes toward a Theory of Education," *Notes on Education,* no. 1, pp. 4–5, Institute of Philosophy and Politics of Education, Teachers College, Columbia University, New York, June 1973.

18 Mina Swaminathan, "The Preschool Child in India," *Assignment Children*, vol. XXI, p. 3, January–March 1973.

19 This statement is based on the number of children below the age of compulsory schooling (our definition of early schooling). In France, where compulsory schooling begins at age six, virtually all children between ages five and six attend publicly supported *écoles maternelles* or private kindergartens, as do 93 percent of the four-year-olds, 72 percent of the three-year-olds, and 22 percent of two-year-olds (Myriam David and Irene Lezine, *Early Child Care in France*, Gordon and Breach, New York, 1974, p. 84). The United States lags behind in noncompulsory early schooling programs. However, it is important to note that kindergarten education for five-year-olds is compulsory in many states; therefore, the percentage of five-year-olds attending both compulsory and noncompulsory schooling is equivalent to that of France.

20 Takanishi, "Early Child Care and Education in Cross-National Perspective," *Review of Education*, vol. I, no. 4, November 1975, pp. 497–507.

21 Ibid.

22 Robert Sears, Eleanor E. Maccoby, and Harry Levin, *Patterns of Child Rearing*, Row, Peterson, Evanston, Ill., 1957.

23 LeVine, op. cit.

24 "Reform and Organization of Education in the Asian Region," *Bulletin of the UNESCO Regional Office for Education in Asia*, vol. IV, no. 2, p. 8, March 1970.

25 Eight countries actually were visited, including observations of six schools in the Republic of China (Taiwan). Since it was difficult to obtain current background information on early schooling in Taiwan, a projected chapter on this country was dropped from the book.

CHAPTER 2

JAPAN

The educational history of Japan can be divided into three broad periods: pre-Meiji (1336–1867), Meiji Restoration (1867–1946), and post-World War II (1946–present).[1] Prior to the introduction of a modern educational system in 1872, Japan's schools were designed for different social classes. In feudal society during the Edo period (1603–1867), *hankô* schools (which taught literary and military arts) were set up for the ruling and warrior (*samurai*) class. In the middle of the Edo period, private schools for children of commoners, *tera-koya* ("temple schools"), taught reading, writing, and arithmetic. By the mid-nineteenth century, there were approximately 50,000 *tera-koya* in Japan.[2] In other private schools (*shijuku*), held in the homes of the teachers, Chinese and Japanese classics, calligraphy, and the abacus were taught. The modern system created in 1872 was built upon this existing network.

In 1868, the Emperor Meiji mandated major political, economic, and social reforms which thrust Japan into the modern world. The Fundamental Code of Education in 1872 created an educational system divided into elementary, middle school, and university levels. Normal schools were also established to train teachers. By 1886, four years of compulsory schooling were required, and rapid growth of secondary and vocational schools followed. In 1907 compulsory education was extended to six years. Institutions of higher education were authorized in 1918. During this period, education was seen as the basis of the national welfare and

NOTE: The assistance of Susumu Shibanuma of the Ministry of Education in gaining perspective on preschools in Japan is acknowledged. He also provided an abundance of material in Japanese. Toshio Yamashita, the president of the Early Education Association of Japan, provided materials on the association. Jiei Ono of Chiba Prefecture Schools also provided Japanese materials which were used in this chapter. Judith Takata Hawkins translated the Japanese materials and conducted the Japanese correspondence. The responsibility for the chapter content and its presentation lies with the authors.

prosperity. It was the duty of the Japanese people to become educated to serve the nation

In 1947, after World War II, the educational system was reorganized into the currently used 6-3-3-4 sequence. The reforms were oriented toward the creation of a democratic nation, based on the ideal of equal educational opportunity. Schools were decentralized to weaken the authority of the Ministry of Education and to increase the autonomy of the prefecture (ken, similar to states) and local communities in education. The curricula, texts, and methods were oriented to the new constitution.

Today, all children aged six to fifteen are required to attend six-year elementary schools and three-year lower secondary schools. Education for this group is free, compulsory, and universal (99.5 percent of the age group were enrolled in 1972).[3] If a child's family cannot afford the costs, grants from the national and local governments provide for lunch, supplies, transportation, and medical care. Admission to upper secondary schools is competitive because of a lack of facilities, while higher education is limited to individuals who pass the highly competitive examinations.

Within the last ten years, the Japanese educational system has come under heavy attack from all sectors. Industry has criticized the inability of the educational system to meet its needs for workers. Parents have become concerned about the widespread practice of private tutoring in order for children to weather competitive examination systems at all levels. Student militancy has been a salient aspect of urban Japanese society, and student leaders attack the system with charges of authoritarianism, hypocrisy, and irrelevance. Thus, a third educational reform is under way, based on the 1971 Central Advisory Council on Education report. Preschool education is an important component of the proposed reforms.

The need for preschool education in Japan is related to several factors. Parents desire earlier entrance to school to prepare their children for an examination system which is closely related to socioeconomic mobility. In some cases, parents attempt to enroll their children in special kindergarten schools which are known to be "training grounds" for entry into the elite schools. Parental interest in education has intensified and produced what national observers call the "education mama" to designate a manifestation of maternal anxiety and striving for children's success in the educational system.

The present-day realities of the highly competitive nature of higher education bring pressure for an academic emphasis in preschool education, in spite of governmental policy to the contrary, since education is seen as a critical channel of social and economic mobility in Japan. The relative prestige of the university (and of particular faculties within it) from which an individual is graduated has major implications for the type of lifetime employment he is able to obtain. Certain businesses or ministries within the government tend to hire graduates of particular faculties or particular universities.

The key thus becomes admission to the appropriate college and department, and competition is fierce. The problem is pushed one step further down the educational ladder. To secure the high school preparation which is most likely to ensure high scores on college entrance examinations, it is necessary to have attended a junior high school which will prepare the student to do well on the high school admission examinations. Thus, this process extends all the way down through the elementary schools to the kindergartens. Many kindergartens admit only those who do well on their own admission examinations or interviews. Elementary school examinations tend to be basic intelligence and readiness tests which may include the three R's. Interestingly enough, although it may be necessary to "pass" an entrance examination for admission to an elementary school of good reputation, the kindergartens do not typically provide instruction in the three R's. In fact, such instruction is very much discouraged by both the government and educational leaders at all levels. Though teachers refrain from teaching the three R's in school, they may tutor their pupils in these subjects on a private basis after hours to prepare them for exams.

Another important factor in the increasing need for preschool education in Japan is related to changes in the structure of the family from extended to nuclear, especially in urban areas. Occupational opportunities for women have also widened, and the need for child-care facilities for working mothers is acute. During the 1960s and early 1970s, a great demand for women workers was created because of rapid economic expansion. There was an increased trend for women with children to enter the labor force. In 1970, 50 percent of the female population of working age were employed; they represented 39 percent of Japan's labor force. Forty-six percent of all women with children under the age of six were in the labor force.[4]

In addition to these societal changes, there have also been changes in the development of the Japanese child. The physical growth of children has greatly increased since the war, partially because of Westernized eating habits. Because of exposure to television and other mass media, children have been developing intellectually at a much faster rate than previously. These changes continue to have an impact on the development of early schooling in Japan.

There are two kinds of preschool institutions in Japan. Kindergartens (*yochien*)[5] are regulated by the Ministry of Education and serve three- to six-year-old children. Day nurseries (*hoikusho*)[6] are administered by the Ministry of Welfare and serve children of working mothers from birth to six years. Each will be discussed separately below.

KINDERGARTENS*

The first Japanese kindergarten was established by the government. It opened on November 14, 1876, and was connected with the Tokyo Girls' Higher Normal School. In 1878, a Kindergarten Training School was organized by the Ministry of Education at the normal school. By 1900, there were 241 private and public kindergartens. In 1910, 6 percent of Japanese elementary school children had received kindergarten training.[7]

These earlier kindergartens were influenced by Froebel and the American kindergarten movement of the same period. According to an 1877 report of the Ministry of Education, the curricular areas covered were life, beauty, and knowledge.[8] Activities included playing with five-color balls, connecting chains, pasting up papers, drawing, working with chopsticks, arranging papers, singing songs, understanding examples, playing with blocks, cutting paper, and performing *origami* (the art of paper folding). However, from the beginning, the American influence was modified to fit the Japanese culture. The goals of the first Japanese kindergarten were expressed in the statement that "the [kindergarten] exercises [the children's] natural sense, develops the waking mind, strengthens their bodies, cultivates their emotion and trains to politeness in language and conduct."[9]

In 1899, Fureberu-kai (the Froebel Association) proposed that the ministry establish the comprehensive kindergarten regulations which remained effective until 1947. These regulations, which became the foundation of the Kindergarten Act in 1926, covered school age, hours, number of children, facilities, purposes, and curriculum. In 1926, the number of kindergartens increased to 1,066 and served 100,000 children.[10] Most of these schools, especially the private ones, were located in urban areas.

*For a detailed description of the history of Japanese kindergartens, see Masako Shoji, "Preschools in Japan," *Education in Japan,* vol. 11, pp. 107–118, 1967.

During the period immediately preceding World War II, the kindergarten curriculum became highly nationalistic. However, during the war, many kindergartens were closed because of heavy bombing and the evacuation of children. Others became wartime day nurseries. At the end of the war, the kindergarten became part of the school system through the School Education Law of 1947.

Kindergartens have grown rapidly since the end of the war. There has been considerable discussion regarding the goals of kindergarten education, especially as specified in the 1947 Education Law. A number of committees have been delegated the task of revising curricula to meet the changing needs of the society and of Japanese children.

In recent years, public demand for preschool education has increased. A 1970 survey conducted by the Ministry of Education indicates that 52 percent of parents desire their children to attend kindergartens, 15 percent nursery schools, and 31 percent either one. Less than 3 percent of the parents did not respond. Lack of accessible facilities appeared to be the primary reason why children did not attend the preschool even though their parents desired them to attend.[11]

Although there have been several attempts to lower the compulsory school age from six to five years, this has not yet been achieved. However, in 1964 the kindergarten promotion program was begun to increase the attendance rate in 1970 to approximately 60 percent of the children who entered primary school. A national subsidy program was created to achieve this goal. As a result, many private as well as public kindergartens were established. However, the discrepancy in fees between private and public preschools is great and provides continuing pressure for increasing the number of public kindergartens.

In viewing the relatively high proportion of children enrolled in preschool institutions (see Table 2.1), it is important to note that enrollments differ greatly by prefecture. For example, enrollment ratios by prefecture (the ratio of the children who attended kindergarten to the total first-grade students) in 1969 ranged from 84.3 to 14.2 percent, a difference of 70 percent.[12] The provision of public and private kindergartens also varies in the different prefectures. Poorer prefectures are less able to provide public kindergartens, while private schools tend to exist in greater numbers in major urban areas. [13]

According to governmental regulations, the maximum number of children in a class is forty. In 1969, the average number of children per class was thirty-four, with an average pupil-teacher ratio of twenty-five to one,[14] depending on the age or developmental level of the child. The minimum number of four-hour school days per year is 220[15]—again with consideration for the developmental stage of the child.

TABLE 2.1   KINDERGARTEN STATISTICS

Year	Schools		Enrollment		Full-time Teachers
	Private	Public	Private	Public	
1939*	1,415	613	176,451		
1949	976	811	228,807		
1959	4,496	2,534	699,778		
1961†	4,638	2,579	557,667	241,418	32,789
1962	4,700	2,677	607,591	248,318	34,763
1963	4,829	2,858	657,410	260,395	37,041
1964	5,048	2,974	772,544	288,424	40,975
1965	5,382	3,169	831,645	300,789	45,193
1970‡	6,808	3,831	1,272,653	402,046	66,579
1972§	7,201	4,544	1,427,500	432,761	73,183
1974¶	7,614	5,024	1,690,505	537,344	81,746

* Figures for the years 1939–1959 from *Organization of Preprimary Education,* International Bureau of Education, Geneva, 1961, p. 171.
† Figures for the years 1961–1963 from Masako Shoji, "First National Institute for Early Childhood Education Research and Experimental Kindergarten in Japan," *Childhood Education,* December 1967, p. 253.
‡ Nobuko Takahashi, "Child-Care Programs in Japan," in Pamela Roby (ed.), *Child Care. Who Cares,* Basic Books, New York, 1972, p. 403.
§ Ministry of Education (Japan), *Preprimary School Education of Japan,* 1973.
¶ Ministry of Education (Japan), *Standard School Survey,* May 1, 1974.

With added interest in the care and education of children, enrollments in kindergarten have increased greatly. In 1973, 6 percent of the three-year-olds, 45.5 percent of the four-year-olds, and 61.7 percent of the five-year-olds were enrolled in kindergartens. When the percentage of five-year-olds in kindergarten is combined with that of those in nursery school (24.6 percent), the percentage of five-year-olds enrolled in preschool facilities includes 86 percent of the age group.[16]

Kindergartens are organized and financed by public authorities (prefectural and local), as well as by private and religious organizations. Private kindergartens are supervised by state authorities and are sometimes subsidized by public funds. The Ministry of Education has general responsibility for the kindergartens. At the local level, public kindergartens are under the prefectural and municipal boards of education. About 80 percent of the public kindergartens are attached to public elementary schools.[17] Others are located in Buddhist temples, Shinto shrines, Christian missions, and other buildings.

Classes are frequently held Monday through Saturday. All kindergartens, whether supported partially by public money or entirely by private funds, charge tuition and various other fees. All are regulated by the Ministry of Education, which sets rules regarding the length of the school year, hours of operation, building standards, equipment, training, number of teachers, the principal, and broad outlines of curriculum.

Japanese kindergarten teachers are a well-qualified group. In 1968, 80 percent were fully certified to teach at this level.[18] Kindergarten teachers receive their training in 321 schools located in the faculties of education at the universities or at teacher training institutions. Teacher certificates are classified as regular (first and second class) and emergency. There is no distinction between first- and second-class certificates except in years of training. Individuals with emergency certificates can be only assistant teachers. Emergency certificates for kindergarten teachers are awarded to upper secondary school graduates who pass a prefectural educational examination. Second-class certificates are granted to junior college graduates, and university graduates receive first-class certificates. In addition, a provisional license can be obtained after completing secondary school and passing a state teaching competency examination. Provisional teachers, like those with emergency certificates, are typically employed as assistants.

The status of kindergarten and primary teachers is similar. Often training of the two groups is conducted simultaneously, since many required subjects are common to both. In state kindergartens, salaries are similar to those of primary teachers. In municipal kindergartens, the salaries are dependent on the municipality and are often lower than those of primary teachers. As in most countries, the teaching ranks are predominantly female.

One of the problems facing kindergarten education is the relatively short service of trained teachers. In 1968, more than 50 percent of the teachers had been teaching less than five years.[19] In addition, most teachers are quite young; in the same year, 40 percent were below the age of twenty-four.[20]

Curriculum standards are issued by the Ministry of Education based on consultation with the School Curriculum Council and scholars and professionals in the field of early education. The National Course of

Study is divided into six areas: health, society, nature, language, music, and art. The goals of kindergarten education as articulated by the ministry include:

1   To promote both physical and mental health, and thus to foster the harmonious development of mind and body
2   To foster respect for the fundamental patterns of behavior in daily life, to develop appropriate social attitudes, to build up emotional harmony, and thus to cultivate the foundations of morality
3   To arouse an interest in nature and social affairs, and thus to cultivate the rudiments of the ability to think
4   To foster the attitude of listening to what others say, to arouse a desire to use such words as can be understood by others, and thus to develop an ability to use words effectively
5   To develop self-expression through creative activities
6   To promote spontaneous activities so as to achieve independence, and to give such care and protection as are needed by children
7   To provide appropriate guidance in accordance with individual differences, by taking into consideration the characteristics of each child's physical and mental development
8   To provide comprehensive guidance based on each child's experience, by making full use of each child's interests and needs
9   To provide appropriate guidance, by taking into consideration the actual conditions of the local community and improving the living environment of the kindergarten
10   To provide appropriate guidance, by paying attention to the characteristics of kindergarten education which are different from elementary school education
11   To develop close relations between home and school and through cooperation with education at home, to raise the efficiency of kindergarten education

Regulations call for the provision of the following equipment: material for outdoor games, building blocks, toys, picture books, piano or organ, simple musical instruments, gramophone and records, materials for drawing and handiwork, gardening tools, and equipment for animals. Audio-visual equipment is recommended. An example of a monthly curriculum plan which is based on the integration of the six areas specified by the Ministry of Education is presented in Table 2.2.

In the National Course of Study, the distinction is made between methods of elementary school teaching and those of the preschool. While in the elementary school, each subject is taught individually, the

TABLE 2.2 MONTHLY CURRICULUM PLAN

Month: April
Subject: Happy kindergarten
Monthly Aim: The children will become acquainted with the various play equipment and the new friends and teachers.
Weekly Aims: 1 They will become used to attending school happily.
                2 They will become happy playing outdoors.
                3 They will learn personal living habits.

Subject	Aim of Subject	Concrete Aims	Main Activities
Health	The children will learn to play happily with play equipment, and they will learn proper living at the kindergarten.	The children will learn where the bathroom, wash basin, drinking fountain, etc., are and how to use them in the proper way.	The children will tour the inside of the kindergarten (lavatory, wash basin, drinking fountain).
		They will learn the safe way to play with the institute's equipment.	They will play on the play equipment (rocking horse, slides, swing, seesaw, etc.).
		They will become interested in body measurements.	They will measure their height and weight.
		They will become able to go to school safely by learning the way to school.	They will learn the way to school.
Society	The children will become familiar with the teacher and the new kindergarten life and happily attend school.	The teacher and friends will come to know the happiness of play, having expectations, and knowing what great numbers of people can do.	They will participate in the kindergarten entrance ceremony.
			They will tour the inside and outside of the school building.
		They will begin to manage the things they have by themselves, understand the names, and know the place where they will leave their personal belongings.	They will learn the appearance of the room, friends, and teacher.
			They will use the greetings "good morning," "good-bye," and "hi."
			They will learn the place to put the things

TABLE 2.2 (continued)

Subject	Aim of Subject	Concrete Aims	Main Activities
			they have.
	They will learn the equipment and the places outside the kindergarten building, and they will use the equipment items carefully without breaking them.		They will freely play with the play equipment.
			They will put away the toys and chairs.
			They will participate in birthday parties during the year. Example of play: sand play, playing horse, etc.
Nature	The children will have an interest in the affairs of the neighborhood and the plants and animals of the kindergarten.	The children will become familiar with the grass and flowers, trees, and shrubs, etc., of the schoolyard, and they will learn not to break or cut them.	The children will look at the flowers in the flower bed.
			They will look at the insects which gather on the flowers.
		They will try to be kind to their animals and not to handle them recklessly.	They will gather flower petals.
		They will learn to open and close doors properly and shut the water faucet tightly.	They will go for walks to the nearby parks and shrines.
			They will observe the animals raised in the kindergarten.
Language	The children will learn to use various greetings and to know the name of the kindergarten.	The children will be able to answer if their name is called.	The children will participate in the kindergarten entrance ceremony and will answer when they are called.
		They will be able to say the names of their friends, the class, and the teacher.	They will use salutations when coming to or leaving the school and for birthday parties ("good morning," "good-bye," "congratulations").
	They will become able to express their own feelings and needs.	They will be able to say various greetings.	

		They will be happy looking at picture books and story shows. They will be able to tell their teacher and friends what they want to do and what they want done.	They will look at picture story shows and books (*Little Black Sambo, Three Little Pigs, Thumbelina*). They will ask the teacher for help when they lose something, when there is illness, and when they have to go to the bathroom.
Musical rhythm	The children will learn to combine songs and music with movement and to sing new songs and familiar songs with friends and the teacher.	The children will happily sing with their friends. They will freely play the hand castanet, accompanied by music. Combining music and song, they will enjoy moving rhythmically while walking, running, and jumping.	The children will sing songs they know.
Drawing and painting	The children will learn to do origami and draw pictures to their own liking with friends and the teacher.	The children will become able to draw freely the pictures they like. They will learn to draw on many drawing surfaces using various colors. They will become able to do origami and draw pictures of flowers blooming in the school garden. They will be happy feeling clay. They will have an interest in beautiful things.	The children will draw freely. They will do origami, such as making tulips. They will play with clay (roll, pull off, knead). They will look at all kinds of green trees, birds, flowers, and sky.

SOURCE: Annual Curriculum Program of Chiba Prefecture, City of Ichihara, Hachiman Public Kindergarten, 1974.

six areas of kindergarten education are presented through children's "actual daily experiences and activities . . . according to their ages and stages of development.[21] In recent years, however, this distinction has been subject to continuous debate, especially in the area of language teaching. According to some Japanese educators, children are capable of learning to read and write at age five. Hence, such subjects can be taught in the kindergartens. However, there is strong opposition to this formal approach, especially among early educators. A statement of this opposition can be found in the "Revision of Kindergarten Educational Schedule," which was developed by a group of teachers, scholars, and administrators: "Kindergarten education has an important meaning to foster the foundation of a person, and it is noted that the basic characteristics are in accordance with the growth and experience in the life of a child, to render general guidance and to foster the foundation to form a desirable person. Kindergarten education is not merely a preparatory course for elementary education. At the present time, there are kindergartens biased towards teaching of knowledge and skill, however, such are not in line with the true aim of kindergarten education."[22]

Observations of the School Day in a Kindergarten

The school day in a kindergarten usually begins at about 8:30 A.M. and ends at approximately 1:00 P.M., with the children eating lunch at school. The children are brought to school by their parents, generally by their mothers, around 8:30 in the morning. The child's first act of the day is to bow to the teacher and greet her. Most school children in Japan carry school bags or satchels, which hold their lunches, pencils, crayons, papers, books, and other school materials. By custom, students of all ages through the university level wear identical uniforms. Additionally, most preschool children wear aprons or smocks and carry a fresh handkerchief, which is either attached to the smock with a safety pin, placed in a pocket, or tied around the wrist.

All preschool teachers are female, although frequently directors of preschools are male. At the beginning of the day, the teacher is likely to be engaged in any number of activities. She might be speaking with a parent, with another teacher, or with her assistant; she might be preparing for activities following the free-play period. However, most frequently, she was observed actively engaged in playing with a group of children from her class. The teacher and her assistant might sit in the sandbox and help construct elaborate rivers and tunnels. Or they might get on the slide with the children or into one of the swings which hold up to fifteen or twenty children. They help catch insects or feed baby dolls. They run relay races, and they play tag. Thus, they participate in, encourage, and enjoy the various activities of the children, sometimes as the leader, making various suggestions or initiating action, sometimes as a follower, but always as a participant. The teachers also answer the children's requests for various kinds of assistance. Unlike teachers in the United States, they rarely spend time settling fights or quarrels. Japanese preschool children, even when left at essentially unsupervised play for up to three hours, were not observed to engage in physical assaults of any kind.[23]

Outdoors, most preschools have jungle gyms and other outdoor climbing equipment of various kinds. There are generally swings, slides, merry-go-rounds, sandboxes, water, and live animals in cages, such as birds, ducks, or rabbits. In addition, plants, tricycles and/or bicycles, balls, pails, and shovels are available. Indoors, there are usually crayons, pencils, paste, watercolors, paper and collage materials, clay or plasticene, dolls, doll dishes and clothes, toy animals, building blocks and interlocking table toys, books, phonographs and records, beads, cars and trucks, rhythm instruments, puppets, clocks, scissors, an abacus, and rulers. Other items of equipment are blackboards, chalk, shelves and cubbies, child-sized tables and chairs, sinks with running water, and bathrooms with either Western- and/or Eastern-style toilets. Almost all schools, and most businesses, have a public address system, which is used to signal the end of various activities.

The end of free play, sometime between 9:30 and 10:30 A.M., is generally announced by music played over the public address system. Children and teachers immediately begin cleaning up and putting away equipment. In many schools, they all then proceed to a gym or hall for the morning assembly, which lasts about a half hour. The children are lined up into neat rows by their teachers, and they stand in line as they sing the school song. This is followed by a "good morning" or greeting song, ending with bowing and a chant. After some words from the headmaster, principal, director, or a teacher, there are more songs, usually involving various hand, arm, and, occasionally, foot movements. These might include or be followed by what the Japanese call singing games—elaborate, graceful, and complex circle dances involving hand, arm, foot, and head motions.

At the end of the morning assembly, the children are lined up again and led by their teachers to their classrooms, with a stop on the way to use the bathroom. Older children are generally not supervised; younger children are both supervised and assisted by the teacher.

Classroom activities usually begin with a teacher-initiated and directed activity, such as art or music. This more formal work begins around 10:00 or 11:00 A.M., depending on the previous schedule, and for two- and three-year-olds it may last for thirty to forty-five minutes. Four- to six-year-olds may work for an hour to an hour and a half. At the beginning of a lesson, each child sits in his assigned seat at a table. The teacher stands at the head of the class or in front of the blackboard and explains what they are going to do. When instructed, the children quickly and quietly go to their cubbies, shelves, or drawers, take out the necessary materials, and return with them to their seats. Generally, all children have the same school-prescribed equipment (boxes of crayons, watercolors, boxes of pens and pencils, sharpeners, pads of paper, scissors, paste, clay tools, etc.), which they brought from home at the beginning of the term. When all the children are seated, the teacher passes out any additional materials necessary for the project, such as origami paper for folding projects, or sticks, beans, and collage materials for other projects.

When instructing preschool children in something new, a Japanese teacher first acts out or demonstrates slowly the entire sequence of steps involved in the project, explaining each step as she does so. She then repeats a very careful, slow, and precise demonstration and explanation of each step, and the children begin to work according to her instructions. The teacher walks around the tables as the children work, assisting them and talking with them. Generally, she pays close attention to the work of each child and encourages each one.

If the lesson is a specific exercise such as paper folding, the teacher sees that all children successfully complete one step before she demonstrates the next. If a child is unable to master the next paper fold, the teacher goes to him and specifically demonstrates it for him. If this is still not sufficient, the teacher gently manipulates the child's hands until he can do it. Then she slowly explains the next step, standing in front of the class and demonstrating. Again, she walks among the tables, looking at the work of each child and assisting where necessary until all have successfully completed that step. The children do not call out for attention. They await their turn quietly or talk to their neighbors until the teacher comes. Or they hold up their hands and their work for the teacher to see. If the teacher is close by, they may call to her quietly.

One class was observed working on a project designed by the teacher to integrate the learning of math, science, social studies, and art. The children would make play money and the items to be sold in a market and, once completed, use them for play and discussion purposes. During the "formal" learning period the teacher brought out the clay vegetables the children had made in the preceding days. The clay vegetables were good representations and were carefully painted. The teacher first talked with the children about the vegetables and admired each one, asking the class for its name and who made it. Then she put some of the models out of sight, keeping only two on the tray. She asked what they were. She then asked the children to try to remember what they were, since she was going to remove one when their eyes were closed. Each time someone correctly identified the missing clay vegetable, the teacher praised that child. Everyone who wanted to answer was given a turn. The game was repeated with three, then four, then five, and then six clay vegetables. Finally, two clay vegetables were removed at a time, then three, and then four, until finally all six were removed, and the children tried to remember all six. Then each clay vegetable was held up, and the children were asked to describe its shape. The children participated in this game as eagerly as they had in the preceding one. This activity lasted about forty-five minutes.

Following this activity the teacher brought out some fresh clay and said that they were going to make "fruit" for the store. Each child took out his clay board and clay tools and was given a lump of clay. The teacher asked the children to name some fruits, and they were helped to distinguish fruits from vegetables. Some children set right to work. Others asked for suggestions of what to make. Children began to ask what certain fruits looked like, and when they could not remember even after discussion with the teacher, she showed them books with pictures of various fruits. The teacher held a book so that the child could study the picture and then showed another picture to another child. Some children made many pieces of fruit, others only one. Most children worked for about thirty minutes, and all the products were clearly recognizable. The children frequently asked the teacher to come and look, and she gave praise as requested. When children requested assistance, she showed them how, either with another piece of clay, with another child's work, or with a picture. She did not do it for them or tell them what to do. As the children finished, they independently and at their own pace put their pieces up to dry, washed their equipment and put it away, washed and dried their hands, and took books from the shelf and sat down to look at them. The children either looked at books or helped set the tables until lunch was served, about ten minutes later.

Both the children and the teachers seemed to share a sense of the importance of successful work. Indeed, the only occasion (other than physical pain or illness) when Japanese children were observed crying in school was during handiwork periods when they were unable to complete a task to their own satisfaction. In all cases, the only recognition given by the teacher or other children was to encourage the child to use his handkerchief and to offer assistance in the completion of the task. If a child continued to cry, he was ignored until he regained self-control. Assistance with the task would again be offered by the teacher. This help was always accepted once the child controlled himself, and he would show obvious pleasure at his final success.

The children were never observed to demand, lash out, or have temper tantrums. The greatest losses of control were silent weeping or sulking, and these were caused by only three things—physical pain, the first day at school, and frustration in the completion of a task. Necessary first aid and gentle, kindly attention are given to the child, but weeping is discouraged.

When the day's project is complete, it is time for lunch. The children collect their things and put them away. They may put their work in their school bags, give it to the teacher, or put it in their drawers, depending on the nature of the project. They then go to the bathroom, use the toilets, and wash their hands. While the children are gone, the teacher and perhaps one or two assistants wipe the tables and, if necessary, rearrange them for lunch. They also put out any luncheon equipment which the school might provide, such as place mats or trays. On the way back to the classroom, each child retrieves her satchel. After hanging it over the back of the chair, she removes her drinking cup, takes it to a sink (usually in the classroom but occasionally in the bathroom), and lines up behind the other children. Each child fills her cup with water (and sometimes a few drops of mouthwash), rinses her mouth, expectorates, rinses her cup, and then returns to the table.

In most schools, the children bring their own lunches from home. If that is the case, the child takes his lunch from his satchel and arranges it correctly on the placemat or tray, setting the chopsticks to one side and his cup with unopened drink toward the center of the table. When his lunch has been opened and set out, he sits in his seat talking quietly with his classmates until all are ready.

If the school provides the lunch, the children either are served by the teachers and assistants or go to the school's kitchen for a tray, which they carry back to their classrooms. In all cases, children bring their own drinking cup, eating utensils (Western or oriental), and a clean folded or rolled and dampened hand towel, which they place on the table. Each of these items has its own special container, which the children return to their satchels before sitting down.

When all are seated, the teacher leads the class in a chant or song, and they all bow to each other. In many schools the children talk to each other quietly while they eat. They seem to carry on quite animated discussions but were never observed to be very noisy. In some cases the teacher sits at the table with the children, eating and conversing with them. In other cases she may leave the room entirely. If the school provides the lunch, her time may be taken up in passing out second and third helpings or in going to the school kitchen for more food.

When a child finishes eating, she wipes her hands on her towel. She takes her cup to the sink, rinses it, fills it, rinses her mouth, expectorates, rinses the cup again, and returns with it to the table. She returns the cup, utensils, and towel to their containers and places them in her satchel. If the school provides trays or place mats, she will take hers and put it in the appropriate place. It is seldom necessary to wipe the table or pick up food from the floor after eating, primarily because Japanese children very rarely spill or drop anything. In the few cases when they did, they appeared embarrassed and quickly cleaned up the mess.

The luncheon period, beginning with the first trip to the toilet and ending when the children have finished eating, usually takes about one hour, generally beginning around 11:30 A.M. and lasting until 12:30 P.M. From 12:30 until 1:00 P.M. the children engage in either free play or organized outdoor games such as relay races. One teacher might organize such a game and be joined by any children in the school who are interested. The rest will play as they like. In relay races, one team does not beat the other. Rather, each child runs his own race and is cheered on by his team. The race is between the two individual runners as representatives of a side or team or group of children. Since this is the case, children join and leave the team as they wish, and there is no need for equal numbers—just an equal starting line and two or more groups.

School ends at 1:00 P.M. in all kindergartens. Just before the time to go home the children put away their toys and equipment. They go to their cubbies or lockers or the cloakroom and get their coats and hats, putting these on as they reenter the classroom and sit in their seats. The teacher speaks to the group, and then they may all sing a farewell song. The teacher says good-bye and bows to them, and they return the greeting and the bow from their seats. They may be lined up by the teacher and led to the shoe-changing area, or they may simply be dismissed. The teacher usually stands in the area where the children are picked up and greets the parents.

DAY NURSERIES*

The first day nursery originated in 1890 through the philanthropic motivations of a couple who operated a private school in Niigata. Since the school's students came from poor families, many brought and cared for their younger siblings in the classes. Because the presence of the children interfered with instruction, a day nursery was opened. During the period from 1890 to 1906, fifteen private nurseries were started to serve working mothers and single-parent families.[24]

In the depression following the First World War, the Ministry of Home Affairs sought to distribute funds to build nurseries for children of working parents. In 1919, the first public nurseries were organized in Osaka and other large cities. By 1938, there were 1,495 nurseries in Japan.[25]

Although the curriculum was often similar in the kindergarten and the day nursery, the main purpose of the latter was to permit parents to work. Unlike the kindergartens, there were no regulations governing the nursery until after World War II. With the coming of the Second World War, all nurseries and kindergartens became war nurseries. Once the war ended, each institution developed separately.

The postwar policy regarding day nurseries is based on the belief that, in principle, children are to be raised in their homes under the care of their own parents or guardians. However, Article 24 of the 1947 Child Welfare Law provides for municipal responsibility to care for children "whose guardians are deemed unable to give adequate care owing to work or illness."[26] Articles 1 and 2 proclaim the government's responsibility for the physical and intellectual development of the child and for the protection of mothers. Under this law, social welfare institutions, such as nurseries, foster homes, children's playgrounds, and child guidance clinics, and free midwife services in hospitals have been established to provide care for infants and preschool children without home care.

*For a more detailed history of the day nurseries, see Shoji, op. cit.

Day nurseries serve children from birth to entry into primary schools. Infant programs (below age three) made up 10 percent of the facilities in 1972. All day nurseries are regulated by the Ministry of Health and Welfare in accordance with the minimum standards for child welfare institutions (Ordinance No. 63 of 1948). The standards include detailed specifications for the physical space and equipment of the infant and nursery rooms (Article 50). Staffing patterns and teacher-child ratios are specified (Article 53) according to the child's age. The nurseries provide essentially the same curriculum and equipment for the three- to six-year-old group as the kindergartens as a result of an agreement between the Ministry of Education and the Ministry of Health and Welfare in 1963. Teachers and parents have meetings at the nursery about three to six times a year. Parents are allowed to visit their children during the day. Under Article 56, teachers are expected to be in contact with parents regarding management, nutrition, health, and other aspects of the nursery.

The costs of the day nurseries are shared by the central, prefectural, and local governments. The national government also subsidizes nurseries sponsored by social welfare organizations. Fees are based on a sliding scale dependent on family income. Families without breadwinners can use the nurseries free of charge.

Staff for the day nurseries are trained in 271 day nursery training institutes in universities, colleges, and junior colleges or in schools for kindergarten teachers. Candidates must be graduates of upper secondary schools. The training period lasts two years .

In addition to public nurseries, there are also day nurseries supported by various industries. Industry-sponsored child care began in the early 1960s. In 1968, 1.6 percent of surveyed companies provided day nurseries on their facilities. The number of these nurseries was estimated to be 2,600.[27] A few are sponsored by unions or employee mutual aid cooperatives. Under the Employment Promotion Projects Corporation, funds for constructing and enlarging day care centers in factories and industrial firms can be obtained. Industry-sponsored child care is not addressed by law but is expected to meet the standards of the Child Welfare Law. Local governments can subsidize the centers as a means of securing the employment of mothers and the care of their children.

Under Article 24 of the Child Welfare Law, infants and children may also be cared for in homes. The number of family day care homes is not known, as typically this system is unreported. In Tokyo, there were reportedly 286 government-approved day care mothers in March 1971.[28]

Since 1961, seasonal nurseries have been provided for children of farming and fishing families. Nurseries have also been established in remote and mountainous regions.

Table 2.3 presents day nursery statistics for the period 1951–1974. In a 1967 survey by the Ministry of Health and Welfare, 60 percent of the children who needed public care were enrolled in day nursery centers.[29] Children with day nursery experience made up 24.6 percent of the school entrants in 1972.

TABLE 2.3   DAY NURSERY STATISTICS

	Schools			Enrollment		
Year	Public	Private	Total	Public	Private	Total
1951*	1,202	2,911	4,113	106,316	236,415	340,731
1961	5,707	4,270	9,977	393,628	264,866	658,494
1962	5,948	4,273	10,221	416,778	275,951	692,729
1963	6,176	4,274	10,450	443,154	319,524	753,678
1964	6,424	4,284	10,708	466,238	315,151	781,389
1965	6,732	4,320	11,053	485,967	319,169	805,136
1970†	8,428	5,039	13,467	649,907	410,650	1,060,557
1974‡	10,332	6,160	16,492	940,976	547,441	1,488,417

* Figures for years 1951–1965 from Masako Shoji, "First National Institute for Early Childhood Education Research and Experimental Kindergarten in Japan," *Childhood Education,* December 1967, p. 253.
† Ministry of Health and Welfare (Japan), *Report on Social Welfare Services,* 1970.
‡ Ministry of Welfare (Japan), "Status of Day Nurseries in 1974," *Social Welfare Statistical Monthly Report,* January 1974.

Observations of the School Day in a Nursery School

The school day begins officially at about 8:00 A.M., but someone is present to open the building and receive the children from 7:00. Although the nursery closes at 4:30 P.M., a teacher stays until all the children are picked up.

Table 2.4 presents a schedule for Japanese day nurseries. The activities are quite similar to those of the kindergartens. Any of the lessons described in the section on kindergartens could also have taken place in a day nursery. Since children at the day nursery arrive earlier in the morning, they usually eat earlier. This is especially true of younger children. Most schools try to give lunch at 11:30 A.M. to children under three years. As in kindergarten, the children have free play after lunch. When each child finishes his lunch in either type of school, he may excuse himself to go outside to play. Then it is time for a nap.

The teacher assists the children in taking off their clothes except underwear and in putting on their pajamas. After the children have changed clothes, they go to the bathroom and then to the resting or sleeping room. This may be a room especially reserved for sleeping or, more generally, the hall where the morning assembly was held, now spread with *tatami* mats covered by children's *futons* or quilts. In nurseries with children two years of age and younger, cribs with rails are provided.

TABLE 2.4 SCHEDULE FOR DAY NURSERY

Time	Activity
7:00–8:00 A.M.	Special activities for early group
8:00–9:30	Arrival; morning checkup; free play
9:30–10:00	Group (school) meeting and physical activities
10:00–11:00	Class activities (twice a week—song, rhythmic play, games in a whole group)
11:00–11:30	Outdoor free play or walk
11:30–12:00 noon	Lunch
12:00–1:00 P.M.	Free play (indoor or outdoor)
1:00–2:30	Nap
2:30–3:30	Class activities (games, picture story show, storytelling)
3:30–4:00	Snack
4:30	Leave
4:30–6:00	Special activities for late group

SOURCE: Hiroshi Urabe (ed.), "Day Nursery Problems in Japan (1967)," in *Understanding Japan, Japanese Education,* no. 21, p. 53, International Society for Educational Information, Tokyo, 1968.

Usually children from several groups will sleep in the same room. The teachers squat, kneel, or sit next to the children as they lie on their quilts and gently pat or rub their stomachs, heads, backs, or legs to quiet them. Each teacher or assistant rubs or pats two or three children near her. Generally, some Western light classical or classical music is played softly on the record player. The teachers move at about five- to ten-minute intervals to different children until all are asleep. One teacher or assistant will remain in the room while the children sleep.

The nap can last up to two hours. At the end of the nap, the teachers turn the music on again, raise the blinds, and move slowly to the children, uncovering and touching each one gently, to awaken them. The waking up is permitted to proceed quite slowly, and as much as twenty minutes may elapse before all are up. As each child awakens, he or she puts on shoes and goes to the bathroom, then to class, where the children's clothes are arranged. The teachers assist the children with dressing and then set out a snack. As the children finish dressing, they fold and put away their pajamas and then rinse out their mouths. The snack proceeds much like lunch but without all the utensils, and when the children have finished, they engage in free play until their parents come to pick them up, generally about 4:50 to 5:00 P.M.

FUTURE DIRECTIONS FOR EARLY SCHOOLING

A third period of reform appears to be in the making for Japanese education.[30] The future of preschool education will be affected by the proposals of the Central Council on Education (CCE) contained in its report[31] in which the major problems for future study relevant to preschool education were specified. These problems include:

1 To study measures for promoting balanced development of preschool education and home education from the standpoint of protection and education of small children

2 As regards the kindergartens and nursery schools, which currently play mutually complementary roles as institutions for preschool education, to coordinate their functions rationally and make their systematic expansion and adjustment in conformity with their respective roles

3 To study the proper roles the national government and local public bodies should play for the diffusion and improvement of preschool education in the future, in view of large regional gaps in the rate of diffusion of preschool education and extreme financial burdens the guardians are obliged to bear at present owing to the large dependence on private kindergartens, even in urban districts which show the higher rate of diffusion of preschool education

4 To study the need and possibility of enlarging compulsory education to the stage of preschool education

The council also recommended that the improvement of kindergarten curricula be based on basic research on preprimary education.

The CCE report generated a great deal of controversy regarding its recommendations. There was opposition to lowering the starting age of schooling, as this would deprive children of essential play and free interaction and would prematurely introduce them into competitive situations. Opposition also emerged with regard to experimentation in the lives of children and families.[32]

With increased public pressure for lowering the compulsory age of schooling, the number of kindergartens must be increased, with the primary objective that all five-year-old children who so wish will have access to a kindergarten. In order to achieve this, increases in aid from the national and prefectural governments would be essential. Private kindergartens compose 70 percent of the kindergartens, and parents pay 2.5 times as much for their services as do parents whose children are in public kindergartens. Hence, the number of public kindergartens needs to be increased. The CCE recommended that the number of individually operated or owned kindergartens be reduced and that they be changed to incorporated kindergartens.

In 1972, a ten-year early childhood education promotional plan was started with the goal of providing kindergarten education for all four- and five-year-olds in the country. Under this plan, kindergarten facilities will be expanded to include 6,000 new schools with 43,000 classrooms. Both public and private kindergartens will be encouraged by national subsidies for administrative costs, facilities, and equipment. There will also be increased aid for low-income families with four- and five-year-old children so that their parents can send them to kindergartens. In 1982, it is anticipated that 17.1 percent of the three-year-olds, 68.9 percent of four-year-olds, and 70.5 percent of the five-year-olds will be enrolled in kindergartens.

Although regulations and financing differ for the day nursery and kindergarten, there is a movement for the two systems to be unified, so that child care and education will be integrated into one system. In 1963, the Ministries of Education and of Welfare issued a joint statement regarding the relationship between the day nursery and the kindergarten. Although it was agreed that the objectives and functions of each were different, it was necessary to consider the impact of lowering the compulsory school age on both institutions. Hence, both ministries recommended that in cases where day nurseries took care of children of kindergarten age, they should provide the educational programs of the kindergarten. In addition, systematic planning regarding the development of both institutions at the prefectural and local levels was urged to favor the expansion of kindergartens for children from four to six years of age. Finally, in order to assure the implementation of the kindergarten curriculum, in-service training was to be provided to care givers in the day nurseries.

The pressure to unify the two systems is justified by the argument that the two separate systems are not compatible with equal educational opportunity under the Japanese Constitution and Fundamental Law of

Education.[33] Children should not be denied access to kindergarten education because of socioeconomic reasons, parents' employment or health, and lack of public facilities.

Integrally related to the call for compulsory education for five-year-olds is the question of the relationship between preschool and primary units. Some advocates of compulsory kindergartens have maintained that the kindergarten unit must remain separate in recognition of its unique educational methods and goals and to avoid an academic orientation in the kindergarten, which is currently in disfavor. However, there remains the concern as to how education based on "play" can be articulated with the academic and non-child-care orientation which exists in the elementary school. This concern was stated in the CCE report.

> There is little dispute on the need, under whatever type of school system, of the period of group establishment education, centering on the life of playing with playmates, for promoting small children's growth, that is, for having them smoothly switch from the stage of their being raised mainly by their mothers' nursing at home to the stage of school education centering on the study of subdivided subjects. And yet, opinions are varied over at what specific age of small children and at what type of establishment such a transitional measure should be taken. . . . It is clear that there is no correlation between the children's growth and the current kindergarten education which strongly repudiates the overrating of intellectual studies, and the education in the first and second grades of elementary school, which lacks the nursing factor. And therefore, whatever sort of structural reforms may be contemplated in the future, the important task may be said to overcome such a defect.[34]

However, the discontinuity in educational experience is not merely seen as a structural problem. It also violates the principle of continuous development, which is supported by a number of research studies on perceptual, cognitive, language, and physical development of Japanese children.[35] Finally, the lack of continuity poses problems for curricula in both units. For example, almost all Japanese children now enter the primary grades with a reading knowledge of the two basic alphabets (*kata-kana* and *hira-gana*) and often of the characters (*kanji*). However, the primary school curriculum still teaches these skills as part of the language curriculum.

Related to the articulation problem is the controversy surrounding the role of formal academic instruction in preschools. Even at its inception the kindergarten was viewed as a prep school for the primary grades. Teachers often taught primary school material in the kindergartens.

Part of the controversy appears to stem from the ideal of "equal educational opportunity." It is feared that by the introduction of academic instruction in the preschool, some children will enter the first level more advanced than others who did not or could not have access to an academic preschool. However, since more than 60 percent of the children at age five are in kindergarten at present, this argument is not a very strong one. Furthermore, by age six (the age of compulsory schooling), more than 80 percent of the children can read simple stories.[36]

Along with the continuing debate just outlined, there is a distinct movement toward the early identification of creativity and the training of talented children, such as in the world-renowned Suzuki method of teaching the violin. This movement receives much personal support from the president of the Sony Corporation. It will be interesting to watch for developments in this area coupled with the observed acceleration in the intellectual development of contemporary Japanese children. While the arguments hinge on the aims of preschool education—the "true aim" traditionally being social and emotional development—it is important to note that chronological age is not the critical issue. The issue is the philosophy and practice of two educational units.

Research and Evaluation

In congruence with the stage of development of its educational system, Japan has been a leader in educational research in Asia. However, among the early education ranks, there is an acknowledged need for more basic research on child development and its relationship to the planning of preschool education. In 1966, the National Institute for Early Childhood Educational Research and an experimental kindergarten were established at Hiroshima University. This institute was the first national center on early childhood education at a national Japanese university. The first research project of the institute included an examination of methods of teaching basic skills in the kindergarten. The research facilities of the institute include a TV system for observing the natural behavior of the children in the kindergarten. It is hoped that the research studies of the institute will be used in governmental policy regarding the downward extension of preschool education to four- and five-year-olds.[37]

A number of studies have been conducted to determine the effects of preschool education. Critically important for scholarly as well as policy reasons, this area is extremely complex. Variables such as family background, the reasons for enrolling in preschools, and the nature of the preschool program—its goals and practices—all act together in influencing the observed effects of preschool experience.

During the sixties, the National Institute for Educational Research conducted a study of the effects of preschool education on the academic achievement and personality of primary school children in three prefectures (N = 26 schools, with 4,276 children).[38] The effects of the preschool experience became less visible as children advanced to higher grades, but positive effects were present during the early primary school years. The effects were most evident in the areas of intellectual development and social interactional skills. However, partially because of the underdeveloped state of socioemotional assessment, effects in these areas were not clear. While a two-year preschool experience was found to be more beneficial than a one-year experience, the effects of a three-year experience were not clear. Children who had attended kindergartens had a better scholastic standing than children who attended day nurseries. However, it was not clear whether this finding reflected the effects of kindergarten education or was related to other nonpreschool factors such as family circumstances. The study provided some interesting and useful information on the effects of preschool education, but the implications of the findings for the expansion of kindergarten education were not obvious. However, on the basis of these findings, the CCE report suggested that preschool education could be started at four years of age.

In addition to the educational research which is conducted by the national institutes, child development and preschool research is conducted at the universities and teacher-training institutions. It is impossible to mention all of the many ongoing projects in this active field. Readers who are especially interested in research should consult the *Annals of the Early Childhood Education Association of Japan* (formerly *Childhood Education*). This association (formerly the Japanese Association of Preschool Education) is the largest and most representative professional association of early educators in Japan. It originated after the war in 1945 and was formally organized in 1948 at the site of Japan's first kindergarten. The association is divided into four areas: theory of development; history of childhood education; systems of early childhood education; and program, curriculum, and evaluation.

There is a growing concern about the quality of life for Japanese children, owing to rapid urbanization and national development with accompanying shortages of safe areas for play, increases in environmental hazards to child health, and changes in family and community life. Hence, preschool education is increasingly viewed as a potentially protective environment for assuring the physical and psychological development of children.

Many of the problems of Japanese preschool education are related to the government's role at the national and local levels. Geographical imbalances in the provision of preschool education and the related threat to equal educational opportunity for this age group are primary concerns. Since 70 percent of the kindergartens are private, there must be increased governmental financing of the kindergartens to reduce geographical imbalance in the distribution of private and public kindergartens.

Japan is clearly a leader in the provision of early schooling not only among Asian nations but throughout the world. The factors which limit the provision of early schooling in other Asian countries—limited resources and the priority placed on universal primary education—are not significant factors in Japan. Hence, the struggle to extend compulsory schooling to Japanese five-year-olds will be watched with continuing interest.

NOTES

1 For a comprehensive discussion of the educational history of Japan, see Tokiomi Kaigo, *Japanese Education: Its Past and Present,* Kokusai Bunka Shinko Kai, Tokyo, Japan, 1965.

2 Public Information Bureau, Ministry of Foreign Affairs, *Facts about Japan, Education in Japan,* October 1973, p. 2.

3 Susumu Shibanuma, "Education in Japan," p. 5. (Mimeographed.)

4 Nobuko Takahashi, "Child-Care Programs in Japan," in Pamela Roby (ed.), *Child Care: Who Cares?* Basic Books, New York, 1972, p. 401.

5 *Yochi* means "infancy"; *en,* "garden."

6 *Hoiku* means "nature," "upbringing"; *sho,* "place."

7 Tsunekichi Mizuno, *The Kindergarten in Japan,* Stratford, Boston, 1908, p. 31.

8 Masako Shoji, "Preschools in Japan," *Education in Japan,* vol. 11, pp. 107–118, 1967.

9 Mizuno, op. cit., p. 32.

10 Ibid.

11 Ministry of Education (Japan), *Educational Standards in Japan,* March 1971, pp. 8–9.

12 Ibid., p. 7.

13 Ibid., p. 6.

14 Ministry of Education (Japan), *Education in Japan,* Tokyo, no date, p. 54.

15 Ibid., p. 56.

16 Shibanuma, op. cit., pp. 4–5.

17 Takahashi, op. cit., p. 403.

18 Eiichi Okamoto, "Preschool Education in Japan," unpublished paper, p. 6.

19 Ibid.

20 Ibid.

21 Ibid., p. 4.

22 Hirotaro Sakamoto, *Explanation of Kindergarten, Education Outline,* Fureberu-kan, Tokyo, 1968. (Translated from Japanese.)

23 Although Bettelheim did not observe any instances of physical aggression among the preschool children, in recent conversations with Takanishi, Japanese early childhood educators expressed concern regarding increasing instances of this behavior and the problem of juvenile delinquency among youths from middle-class backgrounds.

24 Shoji, op. cit., p. 115.

25 Ibid., p. 116.

26 Takahashi, op. cit., p. 400.

27 Ibid., p. 402.

28 Ibid., p. 403.

29 Ibid., p. 406.

30 Hiroshi Azuma, "The Third Educational Reform in Japan," *UCLA Educator,* vol. 17, no. 1, pp. 33–35, Fall 1974.

31 Ministry of Education (Japan), Planning and Research Department, "Interim Report on Fundamental Policies and Measures for the Overall Expansion and Development of School Education in the Future" (Analysis and Evaluation of Advancements of Education in Japan and Problems for the Future).

32 Tatsumi Ueno, "Yoji Kyoiku Gimaka no Shomondai," *Japanese Journal of Educational Research* (Tokyo), vol. 35, no. 35, September 1968.

33 Ministry of Education (Japan), "Interim Report," p. 150.

34 Ibid.

35   Mizuno, op. cit., pp. 33–34.

36   Azuma, op. cit., p. 33.

37   Masako Shoji, "First National Institute for Early Childhood Educational Research and Experimental Kindergarten in Japan," *Childhood Education,* December 1967, p. 255.

38   Noriyoshi Nitta and Shigefumi Nagano, "Effects of Preschool Education on Academic Achievement and Personality of Primary School Children," *Bulletin of the National Institute for Educational Research,* no. 68, The National Institute for Educational Research, Tokyo, December 1969.

CHAPTER 3

REPUBLIC OF KOREA

Up until the late nineteenth century, traditional Korean education was based on Chinese Confucian philosophy as well as on Buddhist traditions. This classical education was confined to male children of the ruling classes and provided a background for obtaining governmental positions. A system of state-supported and private schools flourished. In 1882, a royal decree opened state-supported schools to commoners.

When Christian missionaries arrived at the end of the nineteenth century, they extended literacy to the common people (including women) and spread Christian values and Western ideas. The mission schools introduced several innovations in curricula: popularization of the Korean phonetic script, geography, history, arithmetic, and science.

When the Japanese occupied Korea in 1910, a public education system was developed to convert Koreans into loyal Japanese subjects by transplanting the Japanese educational system to Korea. The language of instruction, texts, and examinations was changed from Chinese to Japanese. Although a large number of public schools were opened, specifically at the primary and technical school levels, discriminatory practices limited the educational opportunities of Koreans. The educational system under the Japanese tended to track Koreans into technical training and lower-level governmental positions. Korean and Japanese students were often taught in separate schools, with greater allocation of resources given to the Japanese schools. Hence, the Japanese population was better educated than the Korean and held most of the bureaucratic positions.

In 1945, the American occupation of Korea began. The Japanese system was converted into a rough approximation of the American system, and Korean was reestablished as the language of instruction. The present educational system was developed, and new textbooks were introduced. However, in 1950, war between North and South Korea ensued, and further educational development was suspended until the armistice in 1953. Since the end of the war, there has been such a tremendous quantitative increase in educational facilities that 95 percent of the school-age children were enrolled in elementary schools in 1970.[1]

Currently, six years of primary education are offered in Korea, beginning at age six. Education is universal, compulsory, and free, although texts and other materials must be purchased by the pupil's family. There are also three-year middle schools (junior high schools) and three-year high schools, divided into academic and vocational streams. Admission to both junior and senior high schools is based on difficult achievement examinations, and only the best pupils are admitted to the academic schools. Since education in Korea is thought to be the primary means of social and economic mobility, there is keen competition in climbing the educational ladder. In this context, preschool education is viewed by middle-class parents as a means of providing their children with a head start in the education competition.

THE KINDERGARTEN*

Preschool education is a relatively new feature of Korean schooling. The first kindergarten was opened by American Protestant missionaries in 1914 at Ewha Women's School. Although preschools then spread throughout the country under church sponsorship, during World War II their number was greatly reduced. However, many were reopened in 1945 at the end of the war.

Articles 146 and 147 of the Education Law of 1949 provided for kindergartens with the objectives of physical, mental, and social development.[2] Article 146 states that the aim of a kindergarten will be to teach and rear children and improve them mentally and physically, and Article 147 provided that as a means of carrying out the aim stated in the foregoing article, kindergartens shall emphasize the following goals:

1   Inculcation of the habits necessary to joyous daily life and harmonious physical development
2   Provision of experience in group living and improvement of habits of group cooperation
3   Development of the beginnings of social responsibility

*The term "kindergarten" is used here to indicate a preschool program with an educational rather than custodial emphasis.

4 Instruction in correct speech and development of interest in stories and in picture books

5 Development of interest in creative expression in music, the dance, and painting

Despite this legislative provision, kindergarten education in Korea is private and limited to children from middle- and upper-class backgrounds. In 1969, the annual cost of private preschool education was $40, while the average per capita income was $150.[3] Preschool education is viewed as providing for gifted children or preparing for compulsory schooling.

Kindergartens serve children between three and six years of age and provide a one- or two-year course. Kindergartens are supervised by the Ministry of Education, which sets broad guidelines for the curriculum (a recommended syllabus for kindergarten education was issued by the Ministry of Education in 1969), the number and qualifications of teachers, the length of the school year (200 days), and hours of operation. According to Ministry rules, the maximum number of children in a class is forty. Generally, two teachers are assigned to a class. Although the schools are supervised by the Ministry, they are financed by the organizers and by fees paid by parents.

Since 1964, an inspection team from the elementary education section of the Ministry makes visits to the Seoul kindergartens each semester. Educational and management plans, equipment, and quality of teaching are checked. The team can recommend that substandard kindergartens be closed.[4]

Since almost all the kindergartens are private, the fees tend to discourage widespread attendance. Approximately 2 percent of the eligible age group attended kindergarten in 1969.[5] In that year, 42.5 percent of the children enrolled were five-year-olds. Less than 8 percent were four-year-olds, and the remainder were six-year-olds.[6] Reasons for this enrollment pattern are due both to financial problems and to the parental view that a two-year preschool education is not essential. Table 3.1 presents kindergarten statistics by year.

One of the reasons for the leveling off of preschool enrollments after 1967, as revealed in Table 3.1, is related to a change that year in entrance requirements for the elite private primary schools. Until 1966, admission to these schools was based on an intelligence test, and parents believed that preschool education would better their children's chances of entering these schools. However, since 1967 students have been chosen by lottery.[7]

Most Korean kindergartens are private and were established by religious groups. Of the 511 private schools in 1971, 225 were founded by Protestants, 118 by Roman Catholics, 12 by Buddhists, and 1 by Confucianists. Of the remainder, 21 were attached to primary schools or to colleges of education, and 127 were established by individuals.[8] The only public kindergarten in 1969 was established by the police department of Choong province. The policemen established the preschool as a preventive measure against juvenile delinquency.[9]

TABLE 3.1   KINDERGARTEN STATISTICS

Year	Schools	Children	Teachers	Number of Children per Teacher
1945*	165	13,534	485	28
1960	297	15,795	1,150	14
1966	499	21,859	1,579	14
1967	468	22,137	1,657	13
1968	470	22,327	1,632	14
1969†	460	21,658§	1,583	14
1970‡	484	22,271	1,660	14
1971	512	22,207	1,694	14

* Statistics for the years 1945 to 1969 are from the Ministry of Education (Republic of Korea), *Education in Korea*, 1970, p. 13.
† In the years 1969–1971, only one kindergarten was publicly supported. This school had an enrollment of eighty children and three teachers in 1969 and 1970.
‡ Statistics for the years 1970 to 1971 are from the Ministry of Education (Republic of Korea), *Statistical Yearbook of Education*, 1971.
§ 9,404 female, 12,254 male.

Kindergarten teachers are required to have fourteen years of schooling, the last two in a specialized course in an education department at the college level. Individuals with a secondary school certificate may enroll in courses in preschool education or nursing which last two to four years. Courses include human growth and development, art in childhood education, children's literature, arts and crafts for teachers, health care of children, kindergarten education, elementary school science, rhythmical expression and games, teaching social studies, child nutrition, preschool music education, parent education, home and family relations, student teaching, and child psychology.[10] In 1971, approximately 70 percent of the kindergarten teachers were licensed.[11] A majority of the licensed teachers had completed between twelve and fourteen years of schooling.[12] While most of the kindergarten principals (usually ministers or priests) are male, almost the entire teaching staff is female.[13] Fifty percent of the teachers are young women between the ages of twenty and thirty.[14]

In a kindergarten class there is usually one adult, including both teachers and assistant teachers, for about every fourteen to twenty children, depending on the specific school. In schools operated by universities or colleges for teacher training there is often one adult for every eight to ten children. Class size ranges from about twenty to thirty-five children. The assistants may be co-teachers, who share responsibility equally, teacher aides, student teachers taking the practicum part of their training, or teachers who work with a "master" teacher in an in-service training program.

In February 1969, the first kindergarten curriculum was set up by the Ministry of Education (Education Ministry Ordinance No. 207). Designed to meet the purposes set forth in the Education Law of 1949 discussed above, it was prepared by the Korean Association for Kindergarten Education, a professional organization composed of teachers. The curriculum is recommended only, and teachers are encouraged to adapt it to local communities and children's backgrounds. However, research conducted by Sang Keum Lee in Seoul indicated that teachers and principals make curriculum decisions which do not consider the legislated purposes of kindergarten education.[15]

The curriculum plan is divided into five subject areas derived from the education law: health, including hygiene, recreation, and safety; social studies, including individual, social, and national life; natural science, including scientific and arithmetic concepts; language arts; and arts. An example of part of the curriculum is shown in Table 3.2. The method of teaching which is recommended is one which encourages spontaneous play and exploration in accordance with the developmental level of the individual child under the guidance of the teacher. Although the curriculum is divided into subject areas, integration among them is stressed. Kindergarten education is aimed at developing "independent individuals with well-rounded personalities."[16]

As indicated by Table 3.2, a great deal of attention is paid to specifying objectives within a subject area. The Ministry curriculum is seen as a model for teachers in local kindergartens to follow in developing similar objectives for their own children. However, as in many educational settings in the world, this is an ideal which is not often attained. In a national survey of kindergartens, S. W. Choo found that all kindergartens include in their curricula free play, singing, picnics, and manners.[17] More than 90 percent include rhythmic activity, drawing, discussion, number concepts, storytelling, and habit formation. Only a few of the kindergartens focus on reading, writing, playing musical instruments, or arithmetic. Students at Ewha Women's University asked teachers to rank important activities in kindergartens. The five most important activities were free play, sharing time, artwork, resting, and singing.[18] A Seoul study conducted by Professor Sang Keum Lee indicated that in a majority of the kindergartens children spend fifteen to thirty minutes a day singing.[19] The following discussion of the school day in a Korean kindergarten is based on Bettelheim's observations.

TABLE 3.2 CURRICULUM FOR KINDERGARTEN IN KOREA—SOCIETY (SOCIAL STUDIES) COMPONENT

Objectives
1 To cultivate the spirit and attitude of independence
2 To develop sociability and the spirit of cooperation through desirable social relationships
3 To arouse children's interests in and concern for community life and to help them develop their understanding of and adjustment to the society

Desired Experiences
1 Caring for oneself
    a To do things independently
    b To carry out simple jobs
2 Handling property carefully
    a To discriminate between personal property and that of others
    b To use public property with care
    c To share property
    d To avoid abusing or wasting property
3 Dealing with regulations
    a To know and observe regulations
    b To distinguish right from wrong behavior
    c To keep promises with teacher and friends
    d To observe regulations governing play
    e To know and observe the regulations of the kindergarten
    f To know and observe regulations of home and community
4 Experiencing autonomy and exerting will power
    a To understand and do right things, distinguish from wrong ones, without coercion
    b To foster habits of expressing feelings honestly
    c To keep friendly relationships with others
    d To play and work enthusiastically until activity ends

    e To share happiness with others

    f To try to please others

    g To be responsible for duties regardless of occasion

    h To help others in need whenever necessary

    i To be responsible for one's own achievement

5 Cooperating with others

    a To understand others correctly and to cooperate if necessary

    b To follow directions of parents and teacher

    c To be kind to others and to be thankful for what others do

    d To forgive others' faults

6 Understanding aspects of society

    a To understand cooperation at home and in kindergarten

    b To have an interest in public organizations and transportation media which are closely related to children's welfare

    c To understand tools and machines

    d To participate willingly and heartily in kindergarten activities

7 Showing respect for the nation

    a To understand the spiritual attitude of singing the national anthem

    b To recognize the national colors and to understand the meaning of the symbol so that a love of the nation will be developed

    c To understand the history and patriots of the nation

SOURCE: A translation of the Korean document: *Curriculum for Kindergarten in Korea,* Ministry of Education (Republic of Korea), February 1969.

OBSERVATIONS OF THE SCHOOL DAY

The typical day in a Korean kindergarten is not significantly different from that found in Japan. Table 3.3 summarizes the daily schedule. School generally begins at 9:00 A.M., and the children are brought to school by their mothers or grandmothers and greeted individually by the teachers as they arrive. As in Japan, the children wear aprons or smocks over their clothes, with handkerchiefs attached. Wearing separate shoes for outdoors and indoors is also the custom here.

As in Japan, the first activity of the school day is free play, during which the children may move freely between indoors and outdoors. This period is generally somewhat shorter than in Japan, lasting only thirty minutes to an hour. The equipment available to the children is likely to consist of outdoor climbing apparatus such as slides, swings, teeter-totters; occasional sandboxes and tricycles; and usually plants and garden tools. Indoor equipment includes child-size tables and chairs, an organ or piano, record player, clock, rulers, an abacus, paper, paints and crayons, paste, pencils, collage materials, interlocking table toys, clay or plasticene, dolls with clothes, toy dishes and utensils, toy animals, blocks of various sizes, a blackboard and chalk, calendars, books, cars and trucks, rhythm instruments, puzzles, and, occasionally, balls, wood-working tools, and dress-up clothes.

TABLE 3.3   SCHOOL DAY SCHEDULE

Time	Activity
9:00 A.M.	Beginning of school
9:00–9:30	Free play (indoors and outdoors)
9:30	Morning assembly or beginning of class
9:30–10:15	Group discussion
10:15–10:45	Snacks
10:45–11:30	Organized activity in art, music, or science
11:30–12:00	Nap
12:00–12:30 P.M.	Free play or group discussion
12:30	End of school

Korean teachers, unlike their Japanese counterparts, were not observed to participate actively in the free play of the children. Discipline, when necessary, consisted of a sharp or disapproving look at the "misbehaving" child. If this failed to inhibit the undesirable behavior, the teacher called the child's name in a mild tone of disapproval. Even more rarely did this second method fail to produce results, but when it did, it was usually sufficient for the teacher to say a few quiet words to the child. Group discipline was usually enforced by hand clapping, whistle blowing, verbal requests for quiet or attention, or waiting accompanied by disapproving looks.

To announce the end of free play, the teacher may simply play some music on a piano, organ, or record player; blow a whistle; or, more frequently, make two short, sharp hand claps. At the signal, the children quickly put away whatever toys or equipment they have been using and proceed to either the morning assembly or the classrooms. If the school has a morning assembly, it is conducted in a manner almost identical to that in Japanese schools. If not, morning greetings are exchanged in the classroom. The children quickly take their places in chairs or on the floor and wait quietly for the teacher to begin.

The first classroom activity of the morning is usually group discussion or "news time." The teacher calls on individual children, who show that they wish to say something by raising their hands. When called on, each child stands, either in place or in front with the teacher, and speaks to the group. The teacher generally asks him a question or comments on what he has said, and the child is given an opportunity to reply. Children relate things which they did with their families, such as visiting relatives. They may also talk about neighborhood happenings such as a fire down the street or about objects which they bring to school to show others. They may talk about a toy, animals, seeing airplanes, or simply what happened yesterday at home. When a child has finished, he resumes his former place. Each participating child performs in the same way. A child who is shy but wishes to speak is helped by quiet prompting and questions from the teacher. The listening children sit silently and almost motionless. If a child speaks without raising his hand, the teacher pauses and silently raises her own hand. If this fails, she indicates that she will call on only those who raise their hands. She then waits patiently, her own hand raised, until all the children conform.

Each morning the group discussion focuses on a particular topic. It might be safety at home, firemen, plants, numbers, or important concepts. Thus, in the course of commenting on the children's news, the teacher slowly directs the discussion toward that topic. If the topic is number concepts, for example, the teacher may ask the children to count how many in the classroom are absent. The children may be asked to classify objects which they brought to school and then to count them. The discussion is interspersed with various children's songs relevant to the topic, some already known to the children and some yet to be learned. Related games which can be played indoors while the children are seated are included. The group discussion period lasts between fifteen and forty-five minutes.

In the schools where a snack is served, the children are generally first dismissed to use the toilets and wash their hands before eating. This is the only time during the day when the children are sent as a group to the bathroom. During other periods they individually request the teacher's permission and then go by themselves. When the children finish in the bathroom, they go to the kitchen or to a centrally located table and get their cups of milk, tea, or chocolate and carry them to a seat of their choice. Child volunteers then assist in passing out crackers, fruit, or other food provided by the school. The teacher joins the children at the tables and converses with them as they eat. In schools with a religious affiliation a prayer is said before the meal. As each child finishes, she puts her things away and engages in various free play activities until it is time for the next formal group activity to begin.

Art activity begins with the teacher's description of the nature of the activity. In the informal periods, the teacher and her assistants set out different art materials from which the children may choose. One table might have clay or plasticene together with boards and clay tools; another may have scissors, paste, paper, and old calendars or magazines for collage work; yet another, crayons and paper for drawing. No tears, fights, or upsets were observed when a child did not get to do what she first wanted. If the table of her choice was full, she would simply accept an alternative activity. This type of behavior was observed throughout Asia. When different materials in different colors were passed out, no child was ever observed to object to what she had received or to demand a different or extra one.

In the informal art activities, as the children work with the materials, the teacher walks among the tables observing the children's work, commenting on it, and giving assistance when requested. For example, in one class the children entered the room and selected chairs at one of the five tables. There were six to ten children at each table. The teacher explained the various activities that they would do during the art period. She put boxes with small pieces of paper and old calendars, glue, scissors, and sheets of drawing paper on one table. She then put play dough on some tables and cans of crayons on others, and a little girl passed out sheets of drawing paper to the children seated at the latter. The children were asked to make pictures of objects they had seen at the museum.

If the children needed help, they called to the teacher, who went to each in turn. At the same time she usually talked to the other children at that table about their work. She went from table to table, answering calls with smiles and conversation. When all the children were deeply involved in their work, the teacher stood at the side of the room, observing the class. As the children finished, some brought their pictures or dough projects to show her. She took each, held it up and admired it, and smiled. At the end of the activity, she wrote the date on the back or bottom of each project. The child might then take his project back to his seat to write his name on it, or the teacher might write the child's description of his project on the back of the paper.

In more formal art periods, the project is usually based on the day's group discussion topic. The teacher begins by explaining the project in detail, demonstrating the procedure step-by-step from start to finish. When the teacher has finished, the children are dismissed to get the necessary supplies from their drawers. Those materials which are provided by the school are then handed out, by either the teacher, her assistant, or child volunteers. The children wait until the teacher tells them they may begin. The new activity is begun once they have all the necessary materials or after the teacher repeats a slow demonstration of the first step. In the latter case, all the children, as in Japan, do the same things in the same order and at the same time. And, if it is a particularly difficult task, the teacher explains and demonstrates each step, using the blackboard to clarify certain points.

In one formal art period observed, the teacher handed out bundles of colored origami paper (about four inches square) to each of four children, who then passed out two sheets to each child. The teacher placed several cans of paste on each table. Then she sat down and played the organ, and all the children sang with her. After one song she stopped the singing, stood in front of the class, and told the children to open their sketch pads, in which one could see various paper-folding, cutting, and pasting projects on earlier pages. They opened to an unused piece of paper and folded the others under the book. The teacher reminded them of the discussion they had earlier in the day on safety precautions which children should take. Emphasis had been placed on fire safety. She asked them some questions about fires and firemen. She then instructed the children to draw a fire engine and to fill it in with pieces of colored paper. To demonstrate, she drew a fire engine on the blackboard, tore up the origami paper, and placed the pieces inside the outline of the fire engine. She answered a child's question and then told all the children to begin their drawings.

The teacher moved from child to child and table to table, bending over, touching the children, and talking to them. She occasionally helped children by tearing paper, pasting down a piece or two, or drawing on their papers. The children were told to draw any background they liked around the fire engine. Some drew backgrounds of houses or flowers. Others drew vehicles, including airplanes.

As the children finished (after approximately forty-five minutes), they put their things away and joined the teacher. Sitting on a small chair encircled by the children, she led them in singing softly so as not to disturb those who were still working. The assistant helped those who had not completed their projects. When most of the children had joined the group, the teacher began to tell a story. Like the majority of teachers observed in this study, she told rather than read the story, acting it out with dramatic expressions of her face and voice and with arm gestures. She told it very quietly, and the children listened spellbound.

In some Korean preschools there is a rest period during the morning. The period varies from ten to forty minutes. The children may simply rest their heads on the tables, or they may lie down on rugs, towels, or blankets spread on the floor in rows. The teacher watches the children to be sure they are quiet and resting, occasionally telling one or another to put his head down or to lie quietly. Music played on a piano, record player, or organ signals the end of the rest period. The nap period may be followed by a period of free play or by any of the activities described above.

The school day ends in all Korean preschools with the children seated in chairs on the floor in a semicircle facing the teacher. Accompanied by music played on a piano or organ, the teacher leads the children in singing various songs, using hand and arm movements. She then tells a story. Sitting quietly, the children appear to be absorbed in the story and almost motionless, except for facial expressions which mirror their interest. Following the singing or the story, the teacher leads a group discussion of the day's activities. This is likely to include some form of evaluation of the day. In some schools, each child is requested to evaluate her own behavior during that day. In others, the children and the teacher exchange evaluations of the day's activities as a whole. During the evaluation, as is common in all group activities, the children must raise their hands if they wish a turn to speak. Calling out for attention is never acceptable behavior.

The period for singing, storytelling, and evaluating takes approximately half an hour. At its conclusion the teacher and children exchange formal good-byes. In schools with a religious affiliation, a prayer is said in unison before the group is dismissed. The children run to their cubbies or lockers to change shoes and gather their belongings before running outside to play until their parents come. Teachers follow the children outside and, as in the morning, greet and talk with the parents as they arrive. The school day usually ends between noon and 12:30 P.M.

DAY CARE SERVICES*

The expansion of day care centers since the end of World War II is due to several factors. First, Korean family structure has been changing from a pattern of traditional large extended families to one of nuclear families. Increased industrial development has created more jobs for a larger

*This discussion is based on Yung Ja Whang, *Introduction to Child-care Service,* Chang Shin Printing Co., Seoul, 1971. (In Korean.)

number of women with young children. Finally, Western ideals of democracy and equality have influenced a slowly changing conception of women's role. These factors have necessitated a network of nonfamilial support systems to provide care to young children.

Until the Child Welfare Law was passed in 1961, day care services were organized as part of the relief programs of the government. The law covered three broad purposes: care and education, correction of defective care situations, and mother-child protection. Thus, the following groups of children were identified as eligible for day care services: children from families in which members were dead or missing, usually as a result of the Korean War; children with working mothers; children whose parents were mentally retarded, addicted to drugs or alcohol, or mentally ill; children who needed institutional care; and children from depressed communities. By June 1970, there were 398 centers serving 32,691 children throughout Korea.

Day care is provided in group settings which provide daily or seasonal services. Sponsorship and financing are obtained through both governmental and private sources. One teacher for ten children is recommended for children below age three. A ratio of one teacher to twenty children is recommended when children are above the age of three.

In 1971, there were three training institutes for day care workers. These were the National Social Worker Leader Training Institute, the Pusan Day Care Teacher Training Institute, which was established by the Swedish Association of Child Relief, and the Mennonite Christian Child Welfare Education Department in Taegu. The length of training varies from three weeks at the Pusan Institute to twenty-one weeks at the Mennonite-sponsored center. The training in all three institutes includes principles of child health and psychology, curriculum, and care-giving strategies. The national and Pusan institutes also focus on training in social work. Table 3.4 presents an outline of a typical training course at the National Social Worker Leader Training Institute.

Child care and education are seen to be the major components of a day care center. The development of a caring plan or curriculum is based on the following four factors: provision of safety, health, food, clothing, housing, and basic socialization in a family atmosphere; the developmental stages of the children; individual differences; and social and economic backgrounds of the children, such as family structure and educational level of parents. However, little is known about the actual implementation of the curriculum by the care givers. Table 3.5 presents a daily schedule for a Korean day care center.

TABLE 3.4 DAY CARE TEACHER TRAINING COURSE (8 WEEKS)–NATIONAL SOCIAL WORKER LEADER TRAINING INSTITUTE

Courses	Class Hours
Child development and behavior	30
Importance of day care service	13
The teacher's role	
Increased needs for women in the work force	
Governmental policies	
Establishment, organization, and functions of day care	
Social work techniques	47
Child guidance	
Group dynamics	
Recreation	
Family guidance	
Case study	
Curriculum methods and activities in day care	200
Health care and first aid	
Preparation of meals	
Planning schedules	
Parent involvement	
Activities—toy making, dancing, nature, society, language, singing, art	

TABLE 3.5 DAILY SCHEDULE OF A KOREAN DAY CARE CENTER

Hours	Activities
8:00 A.M.	Morning greetings Free play
10:00	Snacks, toileting, and health inspection Storytelling
10:40	Group singing, dancing, and body movement
11:00	Free play
11:20	Lunch (bread and soup) Toileting
11:50 A.M.–2:00 P.M.	Nap
2:00–2:30	Waking up, toileting, and dressing
2:50	Snack (cookies and milk) with stories
3:30	Special activities—art, music, dance
4:30	Children begin to leave for home

RESEARCH AND EVALUATION

There are many institutes in Korea which conduct educational research. Of these, the Korean Institute for Research in Behavioral Sciences concentrates its research efforts on child development and test construction. Some of the areas of research inquiry include studies on differential aptitude tests, construction of tests of critical thinking and creativity, and studies of the effects of cultural deprivation on cognitive development.

Although preschool education is in the private sector, it is the subject of an annual statistical survey conducted by the Ministry of Education. Also, in 1969, Professors Soon Il Lee and Eun Wha Lee began a study of educational environments, equipment, and facilities in the kindergartens of Korea. A large number of studies have focused on teacher and parent opinions regarding kindergarten education and curriculum. The department of education at Ewha Women's University includes a preschool section in its *Journal of Education,* which reports on research by the students. Articles which have appeared in recent years include "Family Education for Preschool Children" and "A Partial Study of the Advantages of Kindergarten Education."

At the 1969 Bangkok Conference on Preschool Education, Eun Wha Lee identified five problems facing Korean preschool education.[20] First, as predominantly private institutions, preschools are available for only a limited segment of the child population. Thus, Lee urged that the Ministry of Education establish kindergartens as part of the compulsory public school system to enable all Korean children to have access to preschool experience.

Second, in order for preschools to be based in theory and research, a research organization should be established with the task of informing the government and the public of the importance of preschool education. Research should be directed toward the development of preschool goals and programs with improved curricula, methods, facilities, and equipment consistent within the Korean context. Third, the improvement of teaching quality is essential to improving preschool education. To assure high educational standards, the Ministry of Education should require a four-year higher education as the basis for preschool certification. Fourth, sponsors of kindergartens should not be concerned with the schools solely as money-making ventures. Educational equipment and facilities must be improved, and salaries for preschool teachers increased. Finally, the preschool curriculum must be flexible enough to meet the needs of children from different communities who have different family backgrounds and different abilities. Methods must be selected to meet local situations.

As in Japan, children in Korea are expected to enter the primary grades without formal instruction in the basic skills. Hence, the kindergartens do not teach these skills specifically but engage in various activities to prepare children to acquire these skills. It remains to be seen whether the academically oriented preschool will develop in Korea as it has, for example, in Hong Kong.

In summary, preschools are still relatively new institutions in Korean education. Part of any effort to expand preschools must include strategies to inform parents of the value of preschool education. A survey conducted by Professor S. K. Lee indicates that while a majority of parents send their children to kindergartens with hopes that they will learn good study habits, a significant minority of the mothers (23 percent) replied that they saw no value in kindergarten training. Thus, Korean early educators see education of the population regarding the benefits of kindergartens as a priority. Suggested strategies for "educating" parents have included distribution of home education pamphlets and dissemination of ideas by mass media.

NOTES

1 Korean Overseas Information Service, Korea Background Series, *Education,* 1972, p. 14.
2 Ibid., pp. 31–32.
3 Eun Wha Lee, "Preschool Education in Korea," paper presented at The Bangkok Conference on Preschool Education, 1969, p. 7.
4 Ibid., p. 11.
5 Ibid., p. 4.
6 Ibid.
7 Ibid., pp. 3–4.
8 Ministry of Education (Korea), *Statistical Yearbook of Education,* 1971, p. 22.
9 Lee, op. cit., p. 5.
10 Ministry of Education (Korea), op. cit., p. 125.
11 Lee, loc. cit.
12 Ministry of Education (Korea), op. cit., pp. 125–126.
13 Ibid.
14 Ibid., p. 124.
15 Lee, op. cit., p. 12.
16 Ibid., p. 15.
17 Ibid., p. 16.
18 Ibid., p. 17.
19 Ibid.
20 Ibid., pp. 20–22.

CHAPTER 4

HONG KONG

Hong Kong has been a British Crown Colony since 1841, when the British gained dominion over a number of Chinese ports. Physically, the territory of Hong Kong consists of an island and a piece of a peninsula on the Chinese mainland. In 1973, its population was estimated to be 4.1 million.

The development of educational systems in all British colonies in Asia followed similar patterns. At first, all educational endeavors were left, as in England, to voluntary and philanthropic agencies such as businesses and church groups. Two distinct systems emerged, reflecting the major cultural groups, the Chinese and the British. Those Chinese who wished to educate their children in the Chinese language and tradition either organized village and community groups to import a teacher from one of the larger Chinese cities, or they sent their children to Chinese centers of learning. In addition, some of the British missionary schools admitted Chinese as well as European children. Most charged tuition and fees, though a small number of children received scholarships.

It was the British system, however, that had the greatest influence on the present educational system. The British system was organized and operated by voluntary agencies and was modeled entirely on that of the mother country. The educational program was intended for the elite and focused on literary and character training. Thus, in terms of emphasis, it was similar to traditional Chinese education. Traditional Chinese education emphasized the Chinese classics and history in the same way that British education emphasized English, European, and Greco-Roman classics and history. Emphasis was given also to training in the classical

NOTE: The assistance of Yuen-Yu Tse Bush in the preparation of this chapter is acknowledged.

languages, Mandarin Chinese by the one and Greek and Latin by the other. Both systems focused on training their pupils to be "gentlemen" and of "good character," although what constituted "good character" in China was different from that in England.

The English schools in Hong Kong as well as in Malaysia and India were designed so that a pupil would be prepared for the British examinations and, if he passed, be able to transfer to a school in England or its colonies at any point during his educational career. The schools in the colonies used all or many of the same texts, timetables, syllabi, and methods as the schools of Great Britain. In addition, the British universities composed and annually sent out uniform examinations to the colonies so that overseas students could acquire the same certificates and university degrees as students studying in England. Thus, children in England, Hong Kong, Malaysia, India, and other British colonies prepared for and took virtually the same examinations. Today, in many former c. lonies, the British overseas examinations still provide the basis for promotion and the educational standards for the schools.

Although education in Hong Kong is not compulsory, there is virtually universal attendance at the primary level. There are three types of schools based on sponsorship: schools financed and operated solely by the government, those run by voluntary agencies with government assistance, and those run by private groups and individuals. All schools charge tuition and fees, although schools which receive government subsidies must provide a certain percentage (20 to 45 percent) of their places at reduced or no cost to children of lower-income families. However, books, supplies (including paper and pencils), and uniforms must be supplied by the parents of the students. There are government-subsidized places in secondary schools for roughly 15 to 20 percent of primary school graduates, and they are awarded on the basis of rigorous competitive examinations, which are passed only by the best primary graduates. Other students desiring education beyond the six years of primary school must pay the full costs of their education, provided that they can pass the necessary examinations which secure a place in a public or private school.

The educational system is divided into four levels in addition to the preschools. A six-year primary course is offered in Chinese, English, and Anglo-Chinese schools. Following the first level, there is a five-year program for secondary education also offered in the three types of schools. Then, there is the advanced level, consisting of one to two years of study, which prepares candidates for the fourth level, the institutions of higher education.

PRESCHOOLS IN HONG KONG

Primary education in Britain begins at age five when children enter infant schools. However, since Hong Kong begins primary education or first-level schooling at age six or seven, preschools are often seen as substitutes for the infant schools. There has been a rapid growth in kindergartens during the last twenty years. In 1954, about 17,000 children were enrolled. By 1964, the number of children had increased to 40,000, with the 1973 enrollment at approximately 114,115.[1] In 1969, 53 percent of the estimated population of preschool-age children (four- and five-year-olds) were attending kindergartens.[2] This growth is related to increased interest in the value of early education and to increased participation of women in the work force.[3] Many parents and teachers see kindergartens as the first step in the highly competitive system of formal education. Although the number of kindergartens in Hong Kong has declined recently, enrollment increased during the period 1970-73 (see Table 4.1). The tendency has been for larger kindergartens with better facilities to replace those housed in tenement buildings.

TABLE 4.1 KINDERGARTEN STATISTICS

Year	Number	Enrollment
1970	840	134,858
1971	875	140,960
1972	842	141,466
1973	812	144,115

SOURCE: Education Department of Hong Kong, Triennial Survey, 1970–1973, Government Press, Hong Kong, 1974, p. 32.

Kindergartens vary in size from a one-classroom school of 20 children to a fifteen-classroom school which operates in two daily sessions with a total enrollment of 958 children. Different groups of children attend the morning (9 A.M. to 12 noon) and afternoon (1 P.M. to 4 P.M.) sessions. There are also all-day kindergartens (9 A.M. to 3 P.M.). In 1969, the average pupil-teacher ratio was 38.2.[4]

The institutions for early schooling are the kindergartens and day nurseries, which are regulated by different departments. The Kindergarten Section of the Advisory Inspectorate was established in 1953 and is responsible for the supervision and advisement of kindergartens. The Education Ordinance provides for the registration of these schools. However, the role of the government has remained strictly advisory and facilitative, such as in providing land and low-cost facilities to house the programs. Hong Kong kindergartens typically provide a two-year course for children four to six years of age. However, there are a small number of classes for children under four.

Although day nurseries are under the aegis of the Social Welfare Department, there is currently no legislation governing day nursery operations. The nurseries care for children from two to six years of age. However, a common practice is to have a child in a nursery until the age of four and then if the parents can afford the fees, to place the child in a kindergarten from ages four to six.

There are some general differences between the day nurseries and the kindergartens. First, kindergarten programs tend to be half a day in length, while day nurseries run for the entire workday. Second, nurseries do not typically provide formal academic work, while kindergartens do. However, this difference becomes less important as the child gets older since day nurseries attempt to provide an academic program for four- to six-year-old children in their schedules. Third, nurseries serve mainly children of the lower social classes and, provided that they are nonprofit, receive government subsidies toward the maintenance of each child. Kindergartens do not receive subsidies even though they are nonprofit, and since their tuition is relatively high, they tend to serve children from middle- and upper-class families.

Both kindergartens and nurseries may receive certain capital subsidies, interest-free loans, and free grants of land in the New Territories from the government provided that they are nonprofit. The government also provides free or low-cost accommodations for schools in refugee settlement areas, where there is a great need to care for preschool children. Rooftops and ground-floors are converted into kindergarten classrooms. As one example, the Kwai Chung Resettlement Estate in the New Territories has three ground floor kindergartens which provide 2,096 places in thirty-two classrooms.[5] Similar accommodations are made in government low-cost housing estates and the Hong Kong Housing Society estates. All these schools charge fees, although in cases of hardship only a token fee is charged.

While the Departments of Education and Social Welfare are responsible for the supervision of the preschools, unless a particular school applies for government assistance, it is not subject to government regulation. Those which do apply for funds are subject to inspection, which is chiefly concerned with the financial and safety conditions of the school. There are no rules regarding qualifications and certification of teachers. There are suggested curricula, but they are followed only at the desire of the individual school.

In spite of the relative absence of supervision, most kindergartens and nurseries are similar in their curricula and schedules. This similarity is due in large measure to the fact that pupils must pass entrance examinations in order to gain admission to the better primary schools. Since education is neither free nor compulsory, the competition is exceedingly keen. Many kindergartens themselves administer "entrance examinations" to prospective pupils.

Since 1956, the Kindergarten Section of the Advisory Inspectorate has offered a two-year, part-time, in-service training course to kindergarten teachers. Approximately fifty teachers are trained every two years. In 1970, there were two preservice training programs for preschool teachers in Hong Kong, one for day nursery and one for kindergarten teachers. Teachers in preschools are poorly paid. Untrained teachers receive $25 to $83 per month, while qualified teachers receive $83 to $160 per month (1969 figures).[6] Teachers in the rural areas are paid less.

The lack of adequate training facilities is reflected in the qualifications of the teachers. Table 4.2 presents the number of kindergarten teachers by qualification in Hong Kong.

TABLE 4.2   NUMBERS AND QUALIFICATIONS OF KINDERGARTEN TEACHERS IN HONG KONG

Year	Qualifications		Number
1970–71	University graduates or equivalent	Trained	45
		Untrained	100
	Nongraduates	Trained	682
		Untrained	2,847
	Total		3,674
1971–72	University graduates or equivalent	Trained	52
		Untrained	114
	Nongraduates	Trained	741
		Untrained	3,122
	Total		4,029
1972–73	University graduates or equivalent	Trained	71
		Untrained	142
	Nongraduates	Trained	660
		Untrained	2,896
	Total		3,769

SOURCE: Educational Department, *Triennial Survey,* 1970–1973, p. 124.

A model syllabus for kindergartens has been developed by the education department to guide curriculum and practice. The aims of kindergartens, as outlined in the syllabus, are (1) to foster the all-around development of the child—physically, socially, emotionally, as well as intellectually, (2) to provide training for citizenship, and (3) to provide a good foundation for the child's future learning.[7] The syllabus includes learning activities in the areas of creative activities, play and physical education, language development, number work, science, social studies and social training, health education, and music. Detailed objectives and activities are described for each of these areas.

Regarding practice, teachers are encouraged to stimulate children's learning through stories, games, and play. The basis of content and method is the child's own interests and abilities: "The activity in kindergartens no matter what the content or time limit should be decided by the need and interests of the children."[8] Examples of daily schedules for whole day and half-day sessions are also presented (see Tables 4.3 and 4.4).

As in all countries, the model syllabus represents an expression of valued goals and methods as described by the professional leaders and groups in the field of education. However, as Frances Hon, head of the Kindergarten Section of the Advisory Inspectorate, notes, attainment of these standards has not yet been achieved. There is still too much reliance in the kindergartens on textbooks and on collective class activity versus individual and group work.[9] Approximations toward these standards will involve the training of teachers. However, the high pupil-teacher ratio and other factors such as space limitations are also important considerations in understanding existing classroom practices.

OBSERVATIONS OF THE SCHOOL DAY

Preschools in Hong Kong, whether they are Chinese or English schools, usually open between 8:00 and 8:30 A.M., although they do not officially begin until the morning assembly around 9 A.M. Generally, all the children arrive about ten to fifteen minutes before the assembly, although some may arrive as much as an hour before. The children engage in outdoor free play as they arrive at school. The outdoor play area is usually quite small, and since the total number of children in each school is likely to be between 100 and 300, the play area gradually becomes quite crowded. As a consequence, most schools stagger later free play periods so that only some of the children use the yard at any given time. Outdoor equipment usually includes swings, slides, merry-go-rounds, other climbing apparatus, tricycles, wagons, live animals in cages, and balls. During free play, the teachers observe the children, help them when requested, push merry-go-rounds, supervise lines at the slide, greet arriving children and parents, and talk to one another.

TABLE 4.3 WHOLE DAY SCHEDULE FOR KINDERGARTENS

Time	Activity
9:00–9:15 A.M.	Morning meeting
9:15–10:05	Free activity
10:05–10:25	Conversation and discussion
10:25–10:40	Group play and exercises
10:40–11:00	Snacks
11:00–11:30	Academic lessons (reading, writing, arithmetic)
11:30–12:00 noon	Musical activity
12:00–1:30 P.M.	Lunch
1:30–2:30	Nap
2:30–3:00	Free activity
3:00–3:15	Story and singing
3:15	End of school

TABLE 4.4 HALF-DAY SCHEDULE FOR KINDERGARTENS

Time	Activity
9:00–9:15 A.M.	Morning meeting
9:15–9:35	Conversation and discussion
9:35–10:15	Free activity
10:15–10:30	Story and singing
10:30–10:45	Group play and exercises
10:45–11:05	Snack
11:05–11:30	Academic lessons (reading, writing, arithmetic)
11:30–12:00 noon	Musical activity
12:00 noon	End of school

At about 9:00 A.M., the teachers line the children in single file by classes and lead them inside for the morning assembly. Generally, several or all of the classes in the school gather together in a large room. When the children are seated, either on chairs or on the floor, the teachers and the children exchange formal greetings. This is followed by singing and, in schools with a religious affiliation, prayers and a Bible story. Next may be singing games or chants, which are frequently a sort of nursery rhyme accompanied by rhythmic clapping. Both chanting and clapping are common in schools. The morning assembly lasts about fifteen minutes. At its conclusion, the children are lined up in single file, hands on the shoulders of the child in front, and proceed to their classrooms. Class size tends to increase with age to a maximum of about thirty-five.

In day nurseries, two- and three-year-old children are led as a group, usually between fifteen and twenty per group, to the bathroom before going to their room. The teachers and assistants (*amahs*) aid all children who request or require help with any of the steps involved in using the lavatory and rinsing their hands. They undress children, wipe them, rinse their hands, and dry them when necessary.

When the children enter their classrooms, they are seated at tables or desks. In all-day programs, the children first have breakfast, or, if they have been given breakfast prior to the assembly, they are given a snack before beginning work. The first formal activity of the day, in both nurseries and kindergartens, is usually some number work which lasts from twenty to thirty minutes and, depending on the age of the children and the approach of the school, may be composed of quite a variety of activities.

In some cases, the children practice writing numbers in copybooks which the teacher passes out to them. They may copy the numbers from the board or from numbers that the teacher has written at the top of the page. The teacher walks among the children, pointing out errors, erasing some, and taking a child's hand to guide it so that he forms the number correctly. The children work silently and put both their heads and their pencils down on the desks when they are finished. Whenever small breaches of discipline occur, they are corrected simply by a disapproving look or by calling the child's name softly.

Sometimes counting is the major focus. A large counting frame may be used, with the teacher leading the group in counting by units, fives, and tens. The children and the teacher chant rhythmically as they count the balls on the counting frame while the teacher or a child moves the spheres one at a time from one side to the other. In another instance, the teacher might present groups of objects in various sizes for the children to count—two clocks, three buttons, four dolls, five ducks, and so forth. Some objects, such as the ducks, may then be used to introduce a song about ducks, which might then be followed by a counting song. Finally, the children may chant rhythmically by units, beginning with fives, tens, and so forth. In addition, individual children are usually called on to perform, and those who wish a turn are instructed to raise their hands and wait quietly to be called. This instruction is repeated frequently since the children, eager for a turn, often call out as well as raise their hands.

Following the number period are two twenty- to thirty-minute periods which are devoted to arts or crafts, music, writing, and "assigned" or free play. At the end of these two periods there is usually a trip to the bathroom, followed by lunch or a snack. In the case of two- and three-year-old children, trips by the whole group to the bathroom may occur as frequently as every twenty minutes, depending on the teacher and the school.

For art activities the children sit in assigned places while the teachers pass out the materials. The materials may be the same for all or may vary for different tables. The children may make whatever they like with the materials, although the teachers do demonstrate some possibilities to the children. Usual craft or art materials are homemade play dough, homemade finger paint, crayons and paper, collage materials including various kinds of scraps with paste and scissors, colored paper for folding, and paints and brushes. As in Korea, after passing out the materials, the teacher observes the children's work, commenting and answering requests for assistance. If paint or play dough is used, children are clad in extra smocks or aprons prior to starting work. In Hong Kong, the children do not wear uniforms, but they generally do wear aprons or smocks over their clothes.

Music activities are conducted in the classroom or in another larger room. The activities usually include singing and singing games, dancing, and exercises or movements to various musical cues, such as pitch, rhythm, or speed. Often there are two teachers involved, one who plays the music and one who demonstrates or leads the group. Records, tapes, or piano playing accompany music instruction. Rhythm instruments available to the children include plastic baby rattles and wooden sticks.

The music period usually begins with singing familiar songs, which generally involve various gestures. Often, the songs are sung in English as a means of introducing or increasing the children's command of the English language. Following the songs are singing games and dances, including both Western games such as musical chairs and ring-around-the-rosy, as well as the more elaborate, complex, and delicate dances of the Orient. In addition, singing games are frequently designed as small dramas, the children acting out the various parts. One such game involved the use of dolls—the children cradled the babies in their arms, put them to bed, and sang about and pantomimed the various aspects of housework, cooking, feeding the babies, washing, drying, ironing, and folding clothes.

In another drama, a selected group donned special hats, squatted in a line with their hands on the shoulders of the child in front, and formed a caterpillar. As all the children sang, the caterpillar first lay down and slept on the floor. Then it formed itself into a squatting line as it hatched from the egg and walked, in this extremely difficult position, in time to the music. Then it went to sleep in its cocoon, finally emerging as several butterflies. Each child in the chain was a separate butterfly which detached itself and fluttered about the room. The teachers assisted any child who was confused or had difficulty in performing any of the steps by explanation, demonstration, and manipulation of the child's body. Apparently, at least in school, dramatic play occurs only when suggested by the teachers. That is, play where children take specific roles and act out the parts seems to occur only when the teacher suggests it and when she provides some of the props. Sometimes this is simply done by setting up a "store" or "house" corner and suggesting to a few children that they try it. Other times detailed performances are suggested by the teachers. Whether indoors or out, children were not observed to begin such play without some prior suggestion from one of the adults in the environment. They took it up eagerly, however, whenever it was suggested and assistance was offered.

A common feature of music activities is that at various intervals the children are instructed to place their hands with palms together at the sides of their faces and listen in silence to musical selections. At other times, as the children sit in a semicircle, they are instructed to place their hands on the shoulders of the child on either side, and the whole class sways back and forth in time to the music. One or both of these customs were observed as part of music instruction in all schools visited in Hong Kong. Music period usually ends with the singing of familiar songs.

During a writing lesson, the teacher first ruled a number of squares on the blackboard which were similar to those in the children's copybooks. When all the children had their own copybooks and pencils, she began by drawing a single stroke inside one of the squares on the board. In the next square, she drew the same stroke and added a second one, describing what she was doing. The teacher continued this process, adding one stroke per square until she completed the desired Chinese character. When she finished, the children began to copy from the board. They drew the strokes in the same sequence as those on the board until they completed the character. Each stroke had to be correct. Perpendicular lines had to be almost perfectly so; the same for parallels and other relationships. It was also expected that the relative length of the lines, as well as their relative placement, would be correct. While the children worked, the teacher walked among the desks, pointing out any mistakes and frequently erasing incorrect characters. If a child was having great difficulty, she placed her hand over his as he held the pencil and moved his hand so that he wrote the character correctly. She might repeat this several times with one child. When a child finished the assigned number of repetitions of the character, he simply waited quietly. When all had finished, the teacher wrote in sequence the next character on the board, explaining as she did so. In some lessons observed, the teacher wrote the assigned characters in each child's copybook rather than on the board. In some schools, the children are also taught to write English words and Roman letters, as some primary school entrance examinations require that the children read and write both English and Chinese.

English is taught as a second language in all primary schools and in some preschools. Preschools teaching English usually have a specialist who uses the aural-oral approach, which depends on rote learning, drill, and repetition. The teacher begins with words and phrases and progresses to full sentences. For example, children in a more advanced class are asked, "Are you a boy or a girl?" The individual addressed must answer with a full sentence: "I am a boy [girl]." The question is repeated for each child, and each child must answer precisely and with the correct pronunciation. Failures in grammar or pronunciation are corrected. The teacher addresses requests and questions to the whole class as well as to individuals. She might say, "Please take out your English book and turn to page sixty-eight." As the children respond, the teacher walks around to make sure that all have done it correctly. She tells the class, "Close your book now." She looks to make sure that all do. "Put away your book now." The children do so. She might ask the group questions to which they chorus in unison a full-sentence answer. "Which class are you in?" "Where are you studying?" "What day is today?" "How old are you?" (All Chinese children count their age from the New Year regardless of their exact birthdate, and thus all children born in the same year are the same age.) The children are also instructed in the courtesies of the English language: "please," "thank you," and so forth.

One of the two half-hour periods is a play period. If it is "assigned" play, the children are usually seated at tables and assigned a particular toy to play with. All children sitting at the same table are given the same toy. For example, each child at one table might be given a small pegboard with square holes and a set of brightly colored pegs, while children at the next table might be given handfuls of small plastic animals. Other items might be interlocking toys and puzzles, small dishes, small blocks, trucks, cars, or airplanes. Some of the children, especially very small ones, may be sent to a specified part of the room to play with large blocks or pull toys. During assigned play periods, the teachers observe and comment on the children's activities, and usually at some point they sit at one of the tables and work along with the children near them. If the room becomes too noisy, the teachers quiet the children.

Most free-play periods are held outdoors, where the children play in much the same way as when they arrive in the morning. However, the teachers sometimes organize some of the children for group or team games, and if there are live animals, the children are given something to feed them. At the end of the play period, as at the end of all other periods, with the assistance of the teacher the children put away all the equipment used.

Following two periods of activities, the children are lined up in single file, hands on the shoulders of the child in front, and led to the bathroom. Since lunch is to follow, the teacher supervises even the oldest children to ensure that they wash their hands and dry them. The children are lined up for toilets, then for sinks, then for the towel if the school provides one, then to wait for the rest to finish, and finally to go back to the classroom.

In kindergarten half-day programs, the children bring all or part of their lunches from home. Upon their return to the classroom, the children take their towels, boxes, cups, and lunches from their satchels and place them on the tables in front of their seats. If they did not bring lunch, the teacher selects volunteers to assist in passing out sandwiches. When the food is on the tables, the children and teacher say a prayer together. Then all sit down and, after wiping their hands on their damp towels, begin eating. The teachers do not eat with the children but supervise from a distance while they mark papers or prepare supplies for the next activity. The teachers eat lunch between the morning and afternoon sessions.

In all-day nursery programs the school provides the food. The children are seated at the tables and kept busy with rhythmic chants and handclapping until the assistants come with the food. Then the children stand, and the teacher leads them in a prayer. When the children are reseated, the teacher passes out damp towels, bowls of food, and the necessary utensils. In some schools the children eat as soon as they receive their food; in others they must wait for all to be served. The teachers eat with the children, although they are kept busy supplying seconds and thirds to children who wish them. The hot food plates are collected and then dessert, usually fresh fruit, is passed out. After finishing, each child again wipes his hands on the towel, folds and puts it away, and waits for the rest to finish.

In day nursery programs, at the end of lunch children are taken to the bathroom and are undressed for a two- to three-hour nap. After their nap they have one of the activities which they did not have prior to lunch. This varies from school to school. It could be any number of things, such as music, art, a story, or an English lesson. Those schools which did not have a story in the morning will have some sort of story told, read, or dramatized with visual aids in the afternoon. Art or music will often take place in the afternoon. There will also be an additional period of free play, either indoors or outdoors. The school day ends for all-day programs between 3 and 6 P.M., the last hour or so usually spent outdoors.

The children remain in their classrooms when school is officially over and, after exchanging formal good-byes and bows with the teachers, must stay in their seats. They are dismissed one at a time as their parents arrive, or if they take a bus, they are dismissed by bus group. The teacher remains in the room, constantly reminding the children, who seem to want to form clusters for conversation or play, to remain in their seats. She stays until the last child has gone.

FUTURE DIRECTIONS

Continuing issues of concern in Hong Kong include the aims of early schooling programs and the lack of governmental policy in providing early child care and education. There is strong pressure, especially among parents, for formal education to begin below the age of entry to primary school. Thus kindergartens and, to some extent, day nurseries provide training in reading, writing, and arithmetic. As in other countries, early educators disapprove of the introduction of an academic orientation in preschools. However, the demands of the highly competitive postpreschool educational system appear to be winning, reflecting a situation in which the goals of preschool education are in dispute.

Finally, among the workers in the kindergartens and day nurseries, there is concern about the lack of governmental policy in the development of programs for young children. Within the field of education, governmental priorities have been placed on the development of primary, secondary, and technical education. The government has acted to promote and encourage preschool development, but it has not dealt with the issues of goals, methods, and standards for programs. These issues are not unique to Hong Kong; they are the issues of concern throughout Asia and in many other countries as well, including the United States.

NOTES

1 *Education Department of Hong Kong Triennial Survey, 1970–1973,* Government Press, Hong Kong, 1974.
2 Frances Hon, "Kindergarten Education in Hong Kong," unpublished report, December 1, 1969, p. 2. (Mimeographed.)
3 Ibid., p. 1.
4 Ibid., p. 2.
5 Ibid.
6 Ibid.
7 Education Department of Hong Kong, *The Curriculum of Kindergartens,* revised September 1954. (Mimeographed.)
8 Ibid.
9 Hon, op. cit., p. 3.

CHAPTER 5

THE PHILIPPINES

The Philippines is composed of approximately 7,000 islands spread over a 115,000-square-mile area extending from about 600 miles south of Japan to about 400 miles southeast of the Asian mainland. Eleven of the islands compose approximately 95 percent of the land area. The Filipinos are of the same racial origins as the Indonesians, the people of Malaysia, and the Thais. The population speaks eighty different native dialects. Hence, there are variations among the groups which reflect ethnic and language diversity.

No definite information on the educational system before the Spanish colonial period is available. In the precolonial era the islands were divided into independent states under individual rulers. Education appears to have been under the influence of the priests and medicine men, the first schools originating from the religious institutions which were Malay adaptations of the Hindu and Moslem religions.[1] There is some evidence that the local population was literate in using a Sanskrit or Arabic-derived script. There were also a number of Chinese trading communities located in the islands. Here, as elsewhere, the Chinese communities maintained their own language, culture, and religious practices.

The Philippine Islands were colonized by the Spaniards in 1521. Schools were established shortly thereafter to educate the Spanish children, while the missionaries who accompanied the Spanish soldiers set about converting and "educating" the native populations. The Spanish friars established the first schools, whose primary purpose was religious instruction, with reading, writing, and arithmetic secondary. The predominant methods of instruction were memorization, recitation, repetition, and drill. Supplies were extremely scarce, and reading materials were limited to those providing religious instruction.

Education continued to be largely in the hands of Catholic religious orders until the second half of the nineteenth century. Most schools were designed for the children of the Spanish and Filipino elite. The language of instruction, content, and structure from primary through secondary school was Spanish. There were also local religious orders which attempted to provide the elements of instruction for the people, but they reached only a small minority of the population. Since instruction in these schools was conducted in native languages, transition to the elite Spanish system was difficult.

However, in 1863 the colonial government began to take an interest in the education of the common people by issuing various unenforced regulations and decrees. By the last half of the nineteenth century, the government began to undertake more aggressive support, extension, and control of education. An attempt was made to provide compulsory education for children between the ages of six and fourteen. Spanish was to be the medium of instruction; the content was to be the three R's plus catechism. Social immobility was the lot of all persons not literate in Spanish, since those who were literate in Spanish were exempted from personal labor service and certain taxes. However, none of the schools supported by the government were tuition-free. In addition, most of the schools which were supported by the government and run by religious groups were located in the towns and cities, while the majority of the population resided in rural areas.

At the end of the nineteenth century the Filipinos revolted against the Spanish government and declared the Philippines a republic. The Provisional Constitution established for the first time in Filipino history a separation of civic and religious instruction, with state-supported education becoming completely secular. The republic was short-lived owing to colonization by the United States.

The Americans proceeded to establish a system of mass, free, and public elementary schools for children from seven through eleven years. Based on the American model, the schools utilized American texts and teaching aids and English as the language of instruction. The curriculum was composed of the three R's, handicrafts, nature study, hygiene, geography, civics, and vocational training. For the first time tuition, books, and supplies were free. Children flocked to the schools, and efforts to provide enough schools, classrooms, and teachers could not meet the demand.

In 1935, the Philippines became a commonwealth in the transition to complete independence. Great efforts were undertaken to extend public education until the Japanese invasion in 1942. The Japanese remodeled the educational system, and used Japanese as the language of instruction, so that the primary objective of the schools became the development of loyal Japanese subjects. However, Filipino teachers refused to teach in these schools, and many children were kept away during the war years.

Schools reopened in 1945 at the close of World War II. At that time, the country had virtually to reconstruct its educational system. *Barrio* (village) schools were established in small towns to meet the educational needs of a largely rural population.

The current public school system provides six years of free and compulsory education. In 1962–63, this public system accounted for 95 percent of the country's total school enrollment for these six years. The first four grades are known as primary school and enroll children between the ages of seven and eleven. The medium of instruction during the first two years of primary school is one of the eight major vernacular languages of the islands. English and the national language, *Tagalog*, are taught as second languages. From grade three onward, the language of instruction is English, Tagalog being taught as a second language. The next stage of schooling is a two-year intermediate school. Intermediate schools are frequently separate from primary schools, and in rural areas there may be many primary schools feeding one centrally located intermediate school. However, there are relatively few primary schools to serve the rural population, especially in areas distant from Manila, the capital.

In the Philippines, secondary education lasts four years. Admission to public and the better private secondary schools is by examination, and all the schools charge tuition and fees. Over 60 percent of the secondary enrollment is in private schools. There is also an active program of vocational education at the secondary level for the purposes of national economic development. Roughly 50 percent of high school graduates, or 7.5 percent of all first-grade pupils, enter college. Private institutions of higher learning accommodate 80 percent of the college population.

EARLY SCHOOLING IN THE PHILIPPINES

Preschool education in the Philippines was first organized in 1922 at the Harris Memorial School in Manila. Schooling at this level has always been associated with religious groups which ran the schools under the Bureau of Private Education. Since high fees were charged, only a few privileged children attended preschools. Through its health services, the Department of Health has sought to extend kindergarten education to more children. Other voluntary organizations such as the National Federation of Women's Clubs have given support to preschool programs for children of working mothers and low-income families.

Since preschools are almost all private, the Bureau of Public Schools has had limited involvement in this area. The bureau organized Child Development Study Centers at the regional teacher training schools in the fifties under the leadership of Miguela M. Solis, then superintendent of teacher education in the Bureau of Public Schools. Since then, kindergartens have been increasing in number in the training schools and government-sponsored schools. Recently the national government and the Parent-Teacher Association have jointly established public kindergartens, the former defraying the salary costs and the latter providing facilities and equipment. However, these public kindergartens still compose only about 1 percent of the total number in the country, and they continue to be hampered in their growth by lack of funds.

Interest in preschool education has increased markedly during the past thirty years; enrollment has increased from around 7,547 in 1949 to about 42,033 in 1969 (see Table 5.1). However, less than 1 percent of the preschool-age group (three- to six-year-olds) were enrolled in pre-schools during 1968–69. Most of the children are five- to six-year-olds. Ninety-nine percent of the schools are located in urban areas and are

TABLE 5.1   KINDERGARTEN STATISTICS

Year	Schools	Teachers	Enrollment
1949*	142		7,547
1959	193	450	14,416
1961–62†	225	584	22,780
1962–63	226	633	25,886
1963–64	286	647	29,360
1964–65	308	696	30,492
1965–66	317	744	33,348
1966–67‡	333		36,158
1967–68	365		38,705
1968–69	405		42,033

* Statistics for years 1949-1959 from *Organization of Preprimary Education*, International Bureau of Education, Geneva, 1961, p. 211.
† Statistics for years 1961-1966 from *World Survey of Education*, UNESCO, Paris, 1971, p. 976.
‡ Statistics for years 1966-1968 from Miguela Solis, "Philippine Preschool Today," National Coordinating Center for the Study and Development of Filipino Children and Youth, p. 3. In the years 1964-1969, the number of public kindergartens remained constant (12). During the same period, the number of private kindergartens increased from 299 to 393.

privately operated. In 1966, the Catholic Church ran 78 percent of the private preschools; 20 percent were nonsectarian, and 2 percent were Protestant schools. [2]

In 1966, a network of Children's Centers run by volunteers and community contributions was initiated under the sponsorship of the Rural Improvement Clubs (RIC), a volunteer group. The centers offer rural and low-income mothers courses in child development, day care for their children, and teacher training. The general goal of the program is to promote the health and physical and mental development of the children. The centers are open two to three hours a day, three to five times per week. Children are instructed in their native dialect by a volunteer teacher in community facilities. In 1972, there were 384 operating centers in the country.

The central government of the Republic of. the Philippines supervises, regulates, and inspects all aspects of preschool education as it does all other levels of education through the Bureau of Public Schools and the Bureau of Private Schools. It sets regulations concerning buildings, equipment, teacher training, class size, and curriculum. The two major distinctions between public and private preschools are (1) in most of the private preschools, formal academic work is a common practice, while public schools provide "readiness" training and (2) the minimum number and maximum number of children per class permissible in public preschools are twenty and thirty-five respectively, while in the private preschools these limits are thirty and forty-five. Publicly supported schools are not supposed to engage in formal academic training and have smaller class sizes in order to set an example of good educational practices as they are essentially demonstration schools designed to improve practices in the field of education.

The public preschools account for 3 percent of the total enrollment in preschool programs, and all but one of these public schools are attached to teacher training colleges as demonstration schools. The exception is the kindergarten (Children's Village) attached to the experimental school of the National Coordinating Center for the Study and Development of Filipino Children and Youth as part of a research and development program. All the public preschools, although they receive financial support from the national or local government, charge tuition to cover materials and snacks.

Almost all the private preschools are part of larger private schools which may include all grades from nursery through the secondary level and, in some cases, college. Most of these private schools are operated by various orders of the Roman Catholic Church and are not government subsidized. Private kindergartens or nurseries which are not attached to higher schools are negligible in number. Private preschools usually have two or three sections based on age groupings: a nursery section which enrolls two- to three-year-olds, a lower kindergarten for three-and-a-half- through four-year-olds, and a higher kindergarten for five- and six-year-olds.

Almost all private preschools, with the exception of some with a majority of Chinese children, use English as the medium of instruction. Schools with a large Chinese enrollment generally are bilingual, using both English and Mandarin Chinese as their instructional media. They train children to read, write, and speak both languages.

Select private schools at all levels below the university level are considered by Filipinos to offer an educational program superior to that provided by the public schools. This is partly because public elementary schools offer only half-day sessions, often have classes of up to sixty children, and use the vernacular as the medium of instruction in beginning grades. Thus, all parents who can afford it send their children to private schools. However, competition for admission to the private schools is fierce; less than 5 percent of the total elementary-age population is enrolled in private schools, and only some of these schools are considered "first rate." Since the lower end of all these private schools is the nursery school or kindergarten, the competition for entrance occurs at this level. Once a child has gained admission to the nursery or kindergarten department, he is virtually assured of a place in the attached primary school. Further, provided he does not fail the work at each grade level, he is assured of receiving at least a secondary and, in many cases, a higher education as well. However, if a Filipino child is not admitted at the preschool level, in some schools it is difficult to gain admission to higher levels. Thus, in the Philippines, the motivation of parents in sending their children to preschool is to ensure their access to the educational program in the higher grades, including college.

The situation of competition for admission to better schools is related to one of the controversies in Philippine preschools. This controversy is illustrated by a statement by Doreen B. Gamboa, an early educator: "Out of the concept of a prep school seems to have come the idea that a child goes to kindergarten to prepare for Grade 1 (or to a nursery to prepare for kindergarten or to a grade school to prepare for high school, etc.). A sort of PREP for preparation *ad infinitum!* Then when can a parent or a child discover the joy of childhood learning?"[3] Her comment reflects the fear that preschools will become "racetracks."[4]

Since all preschools charge tuition and fees and some require parents to purchase uniforms and various supplies, most of their pupils are members of the middle and upper social classes. Generally the schools interview both parents and child prior to admission. In addition, oral or written tests may be administered before admission is granted. Consequently, many parents teach their children to count and recognize the letters of the alphabet in English before attempting to enroll them in a preschool program, even though English is not typically the child's mother tongue.

Preprimary teachers are required to have four years of special training after ten years of precollege education. However, teachers with a Bachelor of Science in Elementary Education degree are often hired because there is a lack of trained preschool teachers. The National Coordinating Center for the Study and Development of Filipino Children and Youth (NCCSDFCY) has established summer in-service training courses for teachers who are working in kindergartens. The training course includes child development, program administration, curriculum and instruction, and parent-community relations.

The status of kindergarten teachers is similar to that of their primary school colleagues. Schools prefer single and young female teachers. Male preschool teachers are virtually nonexistent. Some exclusive schools pay their kindergarten teachers better salaries than those received by regular elementary school teachers in the public schools. While kindergarten teachers may teach in the lower primary grades, primary teachers are required to undertake special training while or before teaching at the preschool level.

There are four approaches to curriculum planning in the Filipino kindergartens, all of which are derived from those recognizable world-wide. The Balanced Approach is a child-development approach which takes into account the physical, cognitive, social, and emotional development of the child in order "to help the individual child to develop to his possible optimum in the various aspects of living and growth, an individual who can live happily and usefully within his ability in the society to which he belongs."[5] This approach was developed by Miguela M. Solis, the "mother" of the contemporary preschool movement in the Philippines, and is used in the teacher training schools and in the Children's Village of the NCCSDFCY. In this approach, the kindergarten fosters the development of skills for group living as well as individual potentials through respect for individual differences. A close relationship with parents and the community is encouraged.

In addition to the Balanced Approach, the Montessori Method and the Froebelian Approach are also utilized, the latter by a majority of the schools. Finally, there are schools which focus on the academic preparation of the child for first grade and which base their curricula on one or a combination of the other three approaches.

The Department of Education has guides for determining educational activities based primarily on play, though teachers are free to select materials and experiences suited to the development of the children. Typical program activities include discussion, free play, singing and rhythmic exercises, drawing and painting, folk dancing, dramatic play, sewing, music, and penmanship. Table 5.2 presents a time schedule of kindergarten activities.

TABLE 5.2   TYPICAL PROGRAM OF KINDERGARTEN ACTIVITIES

Time	Activities
8:00–8:20 A.M.	Music or play activities Learning and interpretation of songs Free play, including group games, calisthenics, folk dancing
8:20–8:45	Reading readiness Phonics and alphabet reading, accomplishing reading readiness, workbook
8:45–9:00	Language arts Nursery games, rhymes, songs, stories, conversation
9:00–9:15	Social studies Study of oneself, family and the home, school, church, community
9:15–9:30	Health and science Health inspection, development of health habits and practices Care of pets; study of flowers, fruits, vegetables, and plants Study of weather and sky
9:30–9:50	Recess
9:50–10:00	Rest
10:00–10:20	Writing readiness Learning how to write straight and curved lines, alphabet, names, and numbers
10:20–10:40	Arithmetic Counting, writing, and learning number concepts
10:40–11:00	Work education and arts Clay modeling, construction, creative drawing and painting, and other art activities

SOURCE: F. P. Fresnoza and C. D. Casin, *Essentials of Philippine Educational System,* Abiva, Philippines, 1964, pp. 245–246.

OBSERVATIONS OF THE SCHOOL DAY

The schools usually open around 7:30 A.M. The children arrive, brought by their parents or older siblings or by bus, between 7:30 and 8:00 A.M., which is when the day's work formally begins. All preschool programs are half-day, with some schools offering morning and afternoon sessions for about two-and-a-half to three hours each. The morning sessions end between 10:30 and noon, depending on the policy of the school; afternoon sessions are of equal duration and begin either at 11:30 A.M. if the children eat lunch in school, or about 1:00 P.M. if they eat before school.

In most schools the children immediately enter the classroom and hang up or put away their satchels. In some schools the teacher leads group singing during this time and each child joins the group as he arrives. In other schools the children form clusters or talk or play, either indoors or outdoors, until the formal opening of school. In this case the teachers are usually engaged in preparing various materials for later activities while keeping an eye on the children.

The opening of the day's program differs among schools. In some schools it is marked by a formal ceremony with children lined up outside in front of the flag to sing the national anthem, recite prayers, and exchange morning greetings with the teachers. In other schools, the children are given religious instruction or read a Bible story, preceded and followed by prayers and morning greetings. In yet others, it is marked simply by the recitation of a prayer and a formal exchange of greetings at the end of group singing.

Following the morning greetings, the academic day is generally divided into groups or clusters of activities, each cluster forming an approximately twenty-minute period. The major types of clusters focus on reading or prereading exercises, number concepts, language skills, music, art, and sensory training. The last four categories are conducted in a rather similar manner in both public and private schools. The first two, number concepts and reading, are the areas in which the major and striking differences between public and private preschools manifest themselves. Private schools rely heavily on formal instructional methods, while public schools do not. Most private preschools use English as a medium of instruction; some use Chinese or Spanish. Public preschools often use the vernacular or native language of the children attending as the medium of instruction and teach Tagalog (the national language) and/or English as second languages.

In both public and private schools, various singing games and exercises to music or song follow the morning greetings. Rhythmic chanting and clapping are frequent accompaniments to indoor exercises. In addition, the exercises often include training in spatial concepts such as up, down, forward, backward, right, and left. A major purpose of the singing is to facilitate the growth of the child's second-language vocabulary and to increase his familiarity with its sentence structure. Songs are sung at frequent intervals throughout the day for this purpose, as well as to help alleviate the restlessness of the children. Counting songs of various kinds are also frequently sung.

A Private Preschool

Several typical reading activities for four- to six-year-old children in a private preschool were observed. In one English medium school, the children sat in assigned places in straight rows, either on the floor or in chairs facing the blackboard. The teacher began by writing the letter A on the board. At her request the children chorused the name of the letter, the sound, and an associated word—for example, "A says a as in apple." Then the teacher asked for more words beginning with A. As she made the request, she raised her own hand. The children raised their hands to offer words, and the teacher called on individuals one by one. In some schools the children are required to stand when speaking; in others they remain seated. After everyone who wanted a turn had given his A word, the teacher wrote an E on the board. The same process was repeated for E, and then for each of the remaining vowels. After all the vowels had been presented, the teacher led the group in a song about vowels.

Next, the teacher described a game. If the children hear a word beginning with the letter B, they are to shake or wriggle their hands. If they hear a word beginning with the letter D, they are to fold their arms. The teacher demonstrated the movements she wished the children to make as she described them. She then said "butterfly," and then "daddy," "desk," and "dish." The children made the appropriate motions silently in response to each word. Next, pointing to the letters R and S on the board, she told them to clap when they hear a word beginning with R and to put a finger to their mouth when they hear S. She used the words "rabbit," "sandal," "sailor," and "rosary." The game continued with other consonants and other movements.

Then she told the children to stand and jump five times, which they did, counting in unison at the same time. This was followed by a series of directions: "Everybody face the door," "Face the shelf," "Face the blackboard," "Face the front of the room," "Face the teacher," "Face the window," "Face the door," "Face the teacher's chair," "Face your box." The children complied with each request quietly. At the end, she told them, "Very good, everybody. Sit down, please." The children sat. She then led the group in several songs with accompanying gestures. The purpose of this type of activity, observed in several Philippine schools and in India, was primarily to relieve tension, to let off steam in a highly structured way so that the children do not get out of control but have enough relief from demanding tasks to be able to sit still and pay attention for periods of time. A secondary function is to build vocabulary and concepts in a second language.

At the end of the songs, the children were dismissed, several at a time, to get their workbooks and pencils from their boxes. When all were reseated in straight rows, she told them the number of the page to turn to and wrote the number on the board. The children were instructed to raise their hands, look up, or raise their pencils once they found the correct page. She praised those who were quickest.

Once all the children had found the page, the teacher held up her copy of the workbook and pointed to the first problem. The children were to write the first letter of the name of a pictured object in a specified space. The teacher slowly pronounced the name of the object several times and the children wrote in their books, raising their pencils as they finished. When all had finished, the teacher went on to the next problem. This was repeated for several problems, each involving a word which began with a consonant chanted earlier. For the next several problems the children were to write the first two letters of the name of the pictured object. Again, each word was pronounced slowly and precisely for the children, and the teacher waited until all had raised their pencils before going on to the next problem. These problems completed one page of the workbook.

Next, the teacher led the group in singing several songs with accompanying gestures. Then she held up her workbook and, turning the page, instructed the children to do so also. When all indicated that they had turned the page, she explained the new task. The children had to match upper-case letters in the left column with their lower-case counterparts in the right column by drawing a line between them. She demonstrated the first problem so that the children understood what they were to do. She then repeated the instructions in several ways as the children worked. When they had finished, the children were to write their full name on the top of the page and line up in front of her desk to have their work checked. The teacher corrected both pages of each child's work with a red pen before returning the book to the child. The child could now talk with others who had finished or play various games until all had their work checked. In other classes, the children check their own work at the end of each lesson as the teacher reads off the correct answers.

This group had number work during the next period. The number work was based on the set theory approach in most private schools and was presented much like the reading lesson, with the teacher and the group doing preliminary verbal practice at the board followed by individual work in either printed or homemade workbooks.

A Public Preschool

The following is a description of number work presented in a public preschool to an older kindergarten group of children aged five through six years. For the lesson, the children were seated in a cluster on the floor in front of a large calendar hung on the board. The teacher began by asking the children the day of the week. Many children called out the answer. The teacher raised her hand and waited for the children to do likewise, and then called on one for the answer. Then she asked for volunteers to read the date on the calendar. She called one child to the calendar to point to the month, another to the day of the week, and then another to the year. Then the teacher asked the group to say the full date aloud. The group chorused the day, month, year, and finally the full date. Then the teacher asked another child to go to the calendar and point out again each part of the date. At each of the teacher's requests, the child pointed to the number or word requested. The child was successful, and all the observing children clapped.

The lesson then turned to time. Pointing to a large clock situated high on the wall, the teacher asked the children what time it was. She selected a child to reply, who stood and gave the correct time. The teacher and the group applauded. She then explained to the group that she was going to be a clock, showing which arm was the short hand and which the long, and asked them to try to tell the time according to the position of her arms. Each time she changed the position of her arms, the group chorused the answer. Then she selected a child to set the "clock" to a specified time. The child moved the teacher's arms to the right position for that time. When the child got it right, the others clapped.

Next the teacher asked for two volunteers to draw clocks on the board showing the time six o'clock. As the two children drew, the teacher first sang a song about time and then led the group in singing "Hickory-Dickory Dock" with accompanying hand gestures. By the time the song was repeated once, the children at the board had finished their clocks and gone back to their seats. One of the children had reversed the hands so that her clock read 12:30 instead of 6:00. The teacher discussed the two clocks with the group, pointing out the mistake and asking and answering questions about the correct positioning of the hands and what different lengths mean. As she did so, she wrote 12:30 above one clock and 6:00 above the other.

Next, the teacher wrote two numbers on the board and asked the children which number was greater. Following this she wrote a series of pairs of numbers, asking the group which was greater in each pair. Erasing all pairs but 16–60, she asked for a number which was much less than either 16 or 60. Various children called out answers. She was given numbers such as 5, 10, and 100 but wrote only the correct responses on the board. Then she asked for numbers, one less than 5 and four less than 5. Each time the teacher wrote the number on the board, and it was chorused by the children.

After erasing all the numbers but 5, she wrote the equation $5 + 5 = 10$. She asked the children, "Who can make a story about 10?" Children raised their hands. The teacher called on one child at a time and each offered a different "story," for example, $9 + 1 = 10$, $4 + 6 = 10$, and so forth. As she wrote each story on the board, she asked the group whether it was correct. If it was, she asked for another story. If the story was incorrect, e.g., $3 + 9 = 10$, she took an abacus and asked the child who gave the incorrect story to move the beads one at a time in two groups equal to the two numbers which he gave. The child counted the total and then returned to his seat. The teacher moved the beads as the child did and counted them for the benefit of the whole class and then erased the incorrect story.

After gathering all the possible two-digit correct stories about 10, she wrote $10 - 1 = \_\_$ on the board and asked whether a correct story about 10 could be made by means of subtraction instead of addition. The children chorused the answer. Then a child volunteered to make a

correct story. She went to the board and changed the equation to read 11
- 1 = 10. The teacher and children applauded her performance. The
teacher then led the group in a counting song, and the number lesson
was over.

Reading lessons in public schools are similarly conducted. They
involve the whole group, and the teacher, the blackboard, and various
visual aids are used.

Obviously, both public and private schools do in fact provide
instruction in the three R's. This is not government policy and distresses
those who wish these schools to be in accordance with the policy.
Several factors prevent the public schools from complying fully with the
regulations. One factor is that teachers and directors lack opportunities
to observe and be trained in different approaches. An additional factor is
that the teachers, parents, and directors know that the public preschool
children will have to pass entrance examinations for the private schools
if they wish a first-rate education. All wish to give the children the best
possible chance of success. This real pressure undermines the best
intentions and efforts of even those with the will, talent, and capacity to
do differently. However, it should be stressed that workbooks, textbooks, copying, rote work, and formal pencil and paper academic
training are largely absent from the public preschools in contrast to their
use in private schools. In public schools, there is an attempt to prepare
children for examinations by using more informal approaches.

Additional Activities in Public and Private Preschools

Following reading and arithmetic periods in both public and private
schools, the children are lined up and sent or taken to the lavatory to use
the toilets and wash their hands. When they return, they have a snack,
usually brought from home but occasionally supplied by the school. If
brought from home, each child arranges his food on a placemat on his
desk and stands behind his chair. After a group prayer, the children eat.
The teacher may also eat, or she may merely supervise the group as she
checks work or prepares for another activity. As each child finishes, he
puts his things away and either engages in free-play activities or returns
to his seat, where he must remain until the others have finished. The
same procedure is followed where the snack is provided by the school,
except that the children may be served by the teachers.

Following the snack is a ten- to fifteen-minute period for either recess or rest. Recess may be outdoors or indoors depending on available space and equipment. However, outdoor play is not an especially important part of the preschool program in the Philippines. First, it is often too hot for outdoor play by 9 A.M., even in the winter, and there is some serious risk of heat or sun prostration. In addition, the children spend most of their out-of-school hours outdoors at play because the weather is warm and their dwellings tend to be small. Finally, parents and children tend to regard school as a place to work and learn, not to play. However, if recess is taken outdoors, the available play equipment may include climbing apparatus, swings, teeter-totters, tricycles, sand, and slides. If recess is indoors, there may be blocks, cars and trucks, crayons and paper, picture books, puzzles, and a record player with records. If the period is used for resting, the children simply put their heads down on the desks or tables.

After recess there may be an organized art activity such as painting, using plasticene, drawing, paper folding, or collage work for about twenty minutes. The entire class works on the same type of project, although it may be either an open-ended project with each child making what she likes or an assigned task. In either case, the teacher observes the children as they work and gives assistance to those who request it. In addition, on some occasions Philippine teachers when rendering assistance actually perform or complete part of a task for a child. When they finish, the children put their supplies away in the appropriate places and wipe their work tables.

Following art activities there may be a story, organized games, or a set of sensory training tasks. Stories are read or told by the teacher and sometimes a recorded story is played on the record player. These stories are often used as the basis for a group discussion led by the teacher, or they are sometimes directly related to some other aspect of the work. Organized games are regarded as learning activities, not as play. Games such as "Drop the Hankie," "In and Out the Window," "Hokey-Pokey," and "Follow the Leader" are used for the development of language, social skills, cooperation, muscle control, music, and rhythm.

Sensory training may take several forms. For example, the children might be asked to name the colors painted on cardboard rectangles. Or they might be asked to name various two-dimensional shapes painted on or cut out of cardboard. In either of these cases, the teacher holds up the objects and the group choruses, "That is blue," "That is red," "That is lavender," "That is a triangle," "That is a square," and so forth. Then the teacher names a color or object and asks individuals to pick it out. Each child picks the named card and shows it to the class. The teacher asks, "Is he right?" If he is, the children reply, "Yes, that is blue" and then applaud. If he is wrong, the children chorus, "No, that is yellow," and the child who made the mistake replaces the card and selects a new one until he gets it right.

Another type of training involves sounds. The teacher holds various objects behind her back and hits them together to make a noise. The children try to identify the objects which made the noise. Then the teacher shows them the objects (for example, two spoons or two pencils) and puts them behind her back again. Once the children know what objects she has, she asks them to discriminate which set of objects made of which type of material she is using to make the noise.

At the end of the day, the children are lined up for a prayer, formal good-byes, and dismissal. In some cases the children wait outdoors for their parents, siblings, or the bus. In others they wait indoors, playing with available toys which they put away before they leave. Once the teacher has exchanged formal good-byes with the group, she departs. Generally an assistant or guard may wait with the children until all have gone.

RESEARCH AND FUTURE DIRECTIONS

Research on children and the role of preschool education began in 1941 with a survey of preschools in Manila. After the war, research was focused on the effects of preschool experience on primary school achievement and on development of kindergarten curricula. NCCSDFCY was established in 1963 and was responsible for conducting and encouraging child development research among public and private schools, colleges, universities, and other educational agencies. Their research is seen as the basis for establishing a more effective educational system based on the scientific study of Filipino children.

The research of the NCCSDFCY can be characterized as descriptive and normative in line with its responsibility to provide an empirical base for the development of educational programs. Longitudinal and cross-sectional research has been conducted on the physical, perceptual, moral, language, and artistic (singing and art) development of children.

There have also been efforts to identify gifted children and to develop assessment techniques for the Filipino population. Ongoing research continues in these areas and now includes studies of juvenile delinquency and the effects of nutrition on the development of young children. Within the field of early education, the NCCSDFCY has been conducting the project "The Educational Role of Play in. the Early Childhood Development of Filipino Children, Two to Six Years Old." Findings of research on child development are disseminated through the NCCSDFCY publication, *Philippine Journal of Child-Youth Development.*

NCCSDFCY also conducts a laboratory preschool and elementary school, which serve as a setting both for research and the application of findings. A variety of procedures has been developed to assess behavioral changes in the children. The older kindergartners also participate in a self-evaluation process which reflects areas of creativity, responsibility, economic sufficiency, aesthetic development, moral and spiritual development, intellectual development, physical fitness, international relations, and emotional growth.

Preschools have developed and probably will continue to develop slowly as educational institutions in the Philippines. The country still faces the problem of providing compulsory primary education in the rural areas. The lack of resources allocated to the preschool level of education is reflected in inadequate numbers of facilities and trained teachers. To some extent, preschool education is linked to the parents' conception of the child and his development and the role of early education in affecting the child's future. Except perhaps for the laboratory preschools, education at this level is seen as preparation for entry into schools of excellence and into socioeconomic security.

There are, however, signs that the situation is changing somewhat. The First National Assembly on Preschool Education was held in January 1969 and resulted in moves to incorporate preschool education into the national educational system. The Philippine Association of Preschool Educators and the National Committee of the World Organization for Early Childhood Education (OMEP) were directed to formulate a curriculum guide for preschool education, as well as a college training program for teachers. Finally, the systematic and scientific evaluation of early childhood education was encouraged in order to develop preschool education on the basis of observable behavioral changes in children.

NOTES

1 F. P. Fresnoza and C. P. Casin, *Essentials of Philippine Educational System,* Abiva, Philippines, 1964, p. 6.

2 This discussion is based on Miguela M. Solis, "Philippine Preschool Today," paper presented at the 1969 Bangkok Conference on Preschool Education, pp. 2–5.

3 Doreen Gamboa, "On Kindergartens," *Philippine Journal of Education,* vol. XLVII, p. 494, January 1968.

4 Ibid.

5 Solis, op. cit., p. 7.

CHAPTER 6

MALAYSIA

Malaysia is a multiethnic society formed in 1963 through a merger of the Federation of Malaysia and the British Borneo colonies of Sabah and Sarawak. Singapore was originally a member of the federation, but it seceded in 1965. The population of 10.3 million (1969) is composed of four groups: 44 percent Malays, 36 percent Chinese, 10 percent Indians and Pakistanis, and 10 percent representing sixteen indigenous ethnic groups.[1] Thus, Malaysia is a culturally heterogeneous country in which the ethnic groups, up until very recently, have remained culturally, socially, and economically separate. Within this context, Malaysia has based its hopes for national unity and integration on its educational system through the teaching of the official language—Bahasa Malaysia, or Malay.

During the nineteenth and early twentieth centuries, the different ethnic groups in the country had distinct and separate school systems. Some English schools were originally founded by various missionary bodies, and others were private, profit-making schools. All were based on the British model and used, as far as possible, the same techniques, syllabi, timetables, and examinations as the best British private schools. Before World War II, those who attended the English schools were primarily children of European descent, children of Asian converts to the religion of the groups sponsoring the school, and children of the higher

NOTE: Sister Denise Parquette, chairman of the Malaysian Association of Kindergartens, provided a wealth of information for this chapter. Chew Tow Yow of the Curriculum Development Center of the Ministry of Education provided the proceedings of the 1973 Seminar on Early Childhood Education. We would like to acknowledge also the assistance of Zaiton Bte Osman, bibliography documentation and publications assistant, Faculty of Education, University of Malaya. Chooi-Hon Ho, chief librarian, Lincoln Cultural Center, Kuala Lumpur, provided many valuable contacts for inquiries into preschool education.

social classes of Malays, Indians, and Chinese. Since all the schools charged tuition and fees and expected parents to purchase uniforms, books, and other school supplies, virtually the entire student population came from the higher social classes. However, the religious bodies did provide scholarships and uniforms for a few children.

In the same way that the English schools were geared to synchronize with the British educational system and tradition, the Chinese schools, in which the medium of instruction was Mandarin Chinese, were oriented to the educational system and tradition of China. These private schools were organized and supported by various groups within the Chinese community, such as clubs, clans, and business groups. The schools were mainly nonprofit, in the sense that tuition and other funds raised through voluntary contributions were used only to maintain and improve the schools and to pay for teachers, books, and classrooms. Since there were no Chinese teacher-training institutions in the country, teachers were brought in from China, in the same way that English schools imported teachers from Britain. The Chinese schools taught a traditional Chinese curriculum, emphasizing calligraphy, composition, speech, and the great works of Chinese history, philosophy, ethics, science, and literature, generally known as the Chinese classics. They also taught commercial skills, such as arithmetic, accounting, and book-keeping. After 1911, the Chinese schools abandoned the classic education curriculum and developed one based on ideals of postrevolutionary China. The curriculum was intensely nationalistic and focused on Chinese history and values. These schools created a highly literate Chinese group which was hindered in participation in Malaysian national life because of language barriers.

In both the English and the Chinese schools it was possible for students to pass through a series of examinations and eventually to attend a university or college in the mother country or in one of her colonies. However, the medium of instruction in both types of schools was not typically the mother tongue of many students. Most of the Chinese in Malaysia spoke other Chinese dialects, not Mandarin. Children in the English schools frequently spoke an Asian or another European language. Thus, one of the goals of parents in sending their children to these schools was the acquisition of a valued second language, one which would permit the possibility of attaining further education and security in terms of social and economic status.

For the Indian population, Tamil primary schools were established early in the twentieth century. Tamil is the language spoken in the region of India from which most of Malaysia's Indian population emigrated.

Laws required the owners of the large rubber estates, on which most Indians lived and worked, to establish Tamil schools. The schools taught the elements of reading, writing, and arithmetic in the Tamil language. Since these schools had poor students, they could not afford, like the British and the Chinese schools, to import teachers from abroad. Consequently, most of the teachers were untrained.

Since most Malays are Moslems, their schools were originally organized as Koran schools, in which children were taught to recite the Koran from memory. To be able to repeat the Koran in its entirety from memory is an impressive achievement which brings the individual high esteem and prestige in the Moslem community. Koran schools were conducted in Arabic and Malay. A few Malay-language schools were operated by missionary groups and taught elementary reading, writing, arithmetic, hygiene, agriculture, and home science.

Gradually, all the Malay schools were taken over and supported by the British government in order to create a network of schools for the Malays. All adopted a government-authorized syllabus, which contained roughly the same subjects as the Christian mission schools, and all charged fees. However, only elementary schools were provided. Since secondary and higher education were conducted in Chinese or English and stiff examinations given in those languages had to be passed to gain admission, children who attended Malay elementary schools were essentially excluded from further education.

Until the 1960s, texts, teachers, and curricula in the ethnic schools were almost exclusively foreign in origin and orientation. The communal disorders of May 1969 intensified governmental determination to hasten the unification of the school system along national, multiracial lines. Current government policy toward education, as expressed through its support of elementary and secondary schools, is directed toward universalizing Malay as the official state language. There are presently three kinds of schools:

1 Government or "national" schools are totally supported by the national government. Instruction is conducted in Malay, while English is taught as a second language.

2 "Assisted" schools were originally set up by private groups but are now supported partially by the government, which pays for all recurrent expenditures, including teacher salaries, and 50 percent of capital expenditures. Assisted primary schools may be conducted in Malay, English, Chinese, or Tamil, but they must teach Malay and English. They use the same syllabi and timetable as the government schools.

3 Private schools receive no government support and thus are free to teach

their curriculum in any language. For the most part, the private schools provide a traditional Chinese or English education, enroll a tiny minority of the school-age population, and prepare their pupils for later admission to schools abroad.

Through its support of government and assisted schools, Malaysia now provides nine years of tuition-free education—six years of elementary school beginning at age six and three years of lower secondary school (or junior high). Attendance for the first six years is compulsory in western Malaysia but not in the rest of the country. Upper secondary (or senior high) schools are not free, and admission is based on competitive examinations, in English or Malay, given at the completion of lower secondary education. These examinations also determine whether a student is admitted to an academic (college preparatory), technical, agricultural, or vocational upper secondary school.

EARLY SCHOOLING IN MALAYSIA

Kindergartens in Malaysia began about 40 years ago and are mainly private and located in urban areas. Schools which are not run by various religious groups or by the government are independent profit-making institutions. Since the schools admit children between the ages of two and six years, they serve the function of nursery school for the younger children and of infant school for the older ones. The methods are based on the ideas of Froebel and Montessori and on child development approaches. No curriculum is currently provided by the Ministry of Education. In most schools, the children who attend preschools come from the educated middle and upper social classes. Up until recently, kindergartens were segregated by the major ethnic groups into English, Malay, Chinese, and Tamil schools. However, since governmental policy has dictated the use of Malay as the language of instruction, there has been a noticeable integration of ethnic groups at the preschool level.

Although there are not many preschool programs available, a variety of voluntary and governmental agencies is involved in early child care and education, since preschools are viewed as a means of eliminating poverty and providing equal educational opportunity. Care Centers are organized under the Ministry of Labor and located on estates and rubber plantations in rural areas. In 1969, an act was passed requiring employers to construct a nursery when the number of dependents of the workers exceeds ten children. Children from ages two or three months are brought to simple buildings where they are cared for by an older woman who is paid by the employer. The centers provide primarily for the physical care of the children during the workday (5:30 A.M. to 2:00 P.M.). Regulations cover buildings, equipment, and maintenance, and an adult-child ratio of 1 to 15. Milk is provided as well as monthly physical examinations. However, educational programs are virtually nonexistent in the Care Centers.

Another governmental agency, the Ministry of National and Rural Development, sponsors approximately 102 *Taman Bimbingan Kanak* (TBK) or "gardens to guide children" as part of its community development strategy. Education in the TBK follows the principle of learning through play. Women with seven to nine years of schooling are selected for a five-month training program to work in the TBKs with community children.

Federal Land Development Authority (FELDA) kindergartens were begun in 1970 to meet the needs of working mothers. Groups are typically composed of thirty children who are housed in local community centers. The authority provides subsidies toward the care of the children and for equipment. Private groups provide daily food for the children and training for the teachers. At the end of 1972, there were seventy-four FELDA kindergartens in the country. In addition, a number of other voluntary associations have provided education at this level. In 1969, the Malaysian Voluntary Social Workers Corps began Headstart programs based on the American model. Other women's and youth groups have started their own centers. Finally, a compensatory early education project sponsored by the Ministry of Education and the Van Leer Foundation (of the Netherlands) was started in 1972.

The majority of the Malaysian preschoolers are five years old. Statistical information on the Malaysian kindergartens is limited since they constitute a small and private system. Table 6.1 presents statistics available for the years 1966–1972.

TABLE 6.1   KINDERGARTEN STATISTICS

Year	Schools	Students
1966	139	8,350
1967	200	13,885
1968	285	17,652
1969	308	20,820
1970	349	24,901
1972	483	29,657

SOURCE: Sister Denise Parquette, chairman of the Malaysian Association of Kindergartens, personal communication.

Before 1972, there were no facilities for training preschool teachers. However, many qualified teachers were educated in schools of other Asian or Western countries. In 1972, the Ministry of Education organized a one-year training course in which teachers holding a primary school teaching certificate could be trained in preschool education. However, because of the shortage of teachers at the primary level, most teachers have returned to teaching at this level after their training. The Malaysian Association of Kindergartens holds a number of in-service training courses during school holiday periods.

Since the Ministry of Education has no policy regarding kindergarten education, the actual requirements for teachers are very flexible and left to the discretion of the principal of the individual school. All preschool teachers are female, and any woman holding a Senior Cambridge Certificate with a pass in the national language examination can be selected for preschool teaching.

OBSERVATIONS OF THE SCHOOL DAY

Table 6.2 presents a summary of activities for a half-day kindergarten session. The preschool begins at either 8:30 or 9:00 A.M., with the children beginning to arrive half an hour earlier. The day ends at either noon or 12:30 P.M. There are no afternoon sessions because of hot weather at that time during most of the year. In most schools, the children are required to wear uniforms. Boys wear cotton Bermuda-length shorts (the color established by the school), white short-sleeved shirts open at the collar, socks, and shoes or sandals. Girls wear pinafores of a set color, white short-sleeved blouses, socks, and shoes or sandals. This type of uniform is also worn in the Philippines and Thailand.

TABLE 6.2   SCHOOL DAY SCHEDULE

Time	Activity
8:30–9:00 A.M.	Beginning of school
9:00–9:15	Free play
9:15–10:00	Academic work
10:00–10:30	Snack–Recess (Free play)
10:30–10:40	Rest
10:40–11:30	Academic work
11:30–12:00 noon	Arts and crafts
12:00–12:30 P.M.	End of school

As the children arrive, they engage in either outdoor or indoor free play, depending on the rules and circumstances of the school. The teachers are present but are engaged in making preparations for later activities. Preschools are typically housed in churches, temples, and other community facilities. The outdoor area is likely to be a grassy field which varies in size. The children play games which they can invent or have learned, as the only outdoor equipment available might include a few swings and teeter-totters. Indoors there is usually a variety of equipment, including small blocks, interlocking table toys, puzzles, books, a blackboard and chalk, plasticene, collage materials, paste, coloring books, scissors, paper, crayons, paints, rulers, "Play Skool"-type toys, paper of various types, pencils, copybooks, workbooks, cut-and-paste books, small tables or desks, chairs, and occasionally dolls, dishes, and utensils.

At the end of free play, or when school officially begins, a bell is rung or an announcement is made, and the children put away their things and line up for morning greetings. In some schools the children are marched to a hall or patio for a brief morning assembly. If this is the case, the children remain in lines and chorus "good morning" to their teachers and the headmistress. They are then led, still standing in rows, in a prayer, followed by some songs and exercises to recorded music. Then, row by row, the groups are dismissed to go to their classrooms. In other schools, the children have a formal morning ceremony in their classrooms. The teacher stands before the children, who are either seated in rows or lined up, exchanges a formal greeting with the group, and then leads them in a greeting song or songs, followed by a prayer.

In some schools, the first activity after morning greetings is an inspection of personal hygiene. This generally consists of an examination of hands, fingernails, clothing, handkerchief, neck, and ears for cleanliness and neatness.

A group activity, which frequently begins with a discussion of the day's weather, usually follows. During this discussion, the teacher may use a homemade "weather chart," and a volunteer points its arrows in the correct position after the group has chorused the correct answers about the weather. The discussion which follows is usually "news time." The teacher calls upon one child at a time to rise and give his "news." One tells about a family outing, another about a new puppy. One tells what her cat did; another what his brother did. During the observation one child told about a planned move to a new home. The teacher may comment on the remarks of the individual children or perhaps ask for more information. Another type of discussion is one in which the teacher tells or reads a story which has some sort of moral for the conduct of the daily life of a child, such as the consequences of running away or of being disobedient or selfish. The children are encouraged by the teacher's questions to think about the meaning of the story and to relate it to their own lives.

In Malaysian schools, as in the schools of other countries described, much emphasis is placed on training the children to raise their hands and wait quietly for their turn when individual rather than group responses are expected. In discussion periods, for example, a child is called upon only if he has first raised his hand.

The discussion period lasts for about fifteen minutes and is generally followed by academic work. This period lasts about thirty to forty-five minutes and although focused on one subject area, tends to be composed of several integrated activities. Two examples of these activities follow, one for number work and one for reading. The activities were presented to four- to six-year-old children in two different schools observed at the end of the academic year. Some of the children in these groups were about to enter primary school (standard one) at the beginning of the next semester or school term. Similar activities on a more simplified level are prepared for younger children or for the beginning of the academic year.

The arithmetic lesson observed proceeded as follows. The teacher sat on a child's chair in front of a group of children seated on a rug in a cluster. She had several strings; a number of large wooden beads were on each string, with a knot at the end. In addition, she had a box of loose beads on the floor at her side. At the teacher's invitation, each child got his own string of beads, which he recognized by the color of the beads, and returned to his place on the rug. She began the lesson by asking the children how many beads they each had. All counted the beads on their strings and called out when they finished that they had ten. The teacher held up two loose beads and asked, "How many have I here?" They called out, "Two." She then held up a string that she took from a boy near her, saying, "And how many here?" The group chorused, "Ten." She returned the string to the boy and asked, "Who can give me three tens and four units?" All the children raised their hands. The teacher called on one, and that child stood and collected a string from each of two other children. Taking the three strings in her hand, she went to the teacher's side and handed the strings to the teacher. She then selected four beads from the box and also handed them to the teacher. The teacher asked the child to count the beads by tens and then add the units. She waited while the child counted them out loud and then asked, "How many?" The child gave the answer and wrote it on the blackboard as the other children applauded her correct answer. The teacher then returned the strings to their owners while the selected child put the "units" back into the box and returned to her seat. The teacher then asked for "four tens and five units," selected another volunteer, and the whole process was repeated.

Next, the children took their seats, and the teacher passed out homemade arithmetic workbooks in which she had written out problems for each child. Each problem had, from left to right, several groups of identical objects divided by plus signs, an equals sign, and then a blank space. The children had to count the objects in each group, write the number for each group, and then compute the total. The problems were of varying difficulty depending on the ability of each child. When a child completed his problems, he took his book to the teacher. The teacher had the child stand next to her as she checked the work, talking quietly to him as she did so. If all answers were correct, the teacher wrote new problems for the child. The children worked quietly and waited to have their work checked, staying silently in their seats until the teacher was free. Those who made mistakes on the first part corrected their work and had it rechecked before they were given new problems.

Reading activities observed in an English-language school proceeded as follows. The teacher stood in front of the children, who were seated on the floor in a cluster facing her. She held up a rectangular piece of white cardboard with the letter A painted on it and said, "Look at this. What is it? What is the sound?" The children chorused, "A, apple." An individual child offered the word "ashtray." Then the group chimed in with "A, arrow." The teacher nodded and said "That's right," for each correct word offered by individuals or groups. When they could not think of any more words beginning with A, she held up a card with the letter D and asked them to name the letter and to offer words beginning with the sound. The children chorused, "D, d, duck," and then various children offered some other D words, the teacher saying "That's right" for each correct response. Most raised their hands and waited to be called on before giving their words, but a few just called out. Again the teacher waited until every word that could be thought of was offered before going on to the next letter, H.

Then, the teacher pointed to the blackboard, on which she had drawn balloons, each with a lowercase letter written inside. She asked,

"What have we here?" and the children chorused, "Balloons." The teacher said, "That's right. Let's burst the balloons. Can you burst the balloon with the letter g?" Children raised their hands, and she called on one. She handed him a long rubber-tipped pointer, which he used to touch the balloon containing the letter g. All the observing children clapped. The child returned the pointer to the teacher and resumed his seat. The teacher then asked, "Can you burst the balloon with the letter b?" and selected another volunteer. The teacher eventually repeated some of the letters in order to give every child a turn, as they were all eager to participate and appeared to enjoy the game.

Then the teacher asked, "Did we burst all the balloons?" The children suggested omissions, and the teacher asked the group, "Who did this one?" Those who burst that one raised their hands. One child correctly offered the balloon which had been omitted and was given the opportunity to burst it. This was one of many similar types of exercises for training memory and observation skills which are employed frequently in Malaysia, the Philippines, and Thailand.

The lesson concluded with drawing "a picture of a word that begins with D." The teacher asked for suggestions of words beginning with D that they might draw and received many replies. She then instructed a few children at a time to get their crayons from their individual drawers while she placed several sheets of paper on each table. When all were in their seats with the necessary supplies, she said, "You may start drawing now," and the children began.

As the children worked, the teacher walked among the tables, responding to their requests, assisting when asked to, and observing their work. In this class the children talked to each other quietly while they worked, but they were not permitted to leave their seats. In some classes and schools, the children must do all their work in complete silence. The teacher or principal appears to decide whether to expect or to enforce silence, and there is no uniformity of practice in this regard. Children who speak or leave their seats when they should not are first given a disapproving look; if this fails, their names are called; if this still fails, the teacher tells them precisely what is wanted—"No talking, please," "A little less noise, please," or " Quietly, please."

In schools with running water, the morning academic activity is followed by a trip to the lavatory. In some schools the teacher accompanies the children and supervises them in their use of the bathroom. In others, the children go on their own. In schools without running water there is either a potty in a screened-off area of the room or building or, in some cases, an outhouse. There is no group trip to the facility. The children ask the teacher's permission individually to use it. After using the lavatory, the children, if they have gone in a group, return in silence to their classroom, either marching in single file, hands on the shoulders of the child in front, or walking back one at a time.

Snack time usually begins at 10:00 or 10:15 A.M. Each child brings his own snack from home in a satchel. After retrieving it from his shelf or cubby, he takes his place at a table or, in some schools, outdoors. The teacher then leads the children in a prayer, and they begin eating and drinking. The teacher eats her snack either at her desk (in Malaysian preschools the teachers generally have an adult-size desk and chair in some part of the room) or at a table with the children. When the children finish eating, they put their things away.

In some schools, the children may run outdoors for free play or recess as soon as they have put their things away. In others, the children are permitted to get books and look at them silently until the rest finish. In this case, the group is lined up single file and led to the outdoor play area. Recess, or free play, lasts for about twenty minutes. In many schools, the teachers take a break at this time, and either the children play unsupervised or the teachers or assistants take turns supervising, one on duty each day. In a few cases where there is no outdoor equipment, the teachers organize group games of various sorts for those who wish to participate. If the children were lined up to go outside, they are lined up again to come back. If they simply went out as they finished, or ate outside, they go in individually and in clusters when a bell rings or when they are told that recess is over.

Rest period follows free play. In some schools the children lie down on a rug on the floor, while in others the children remain in their seats and rest their heads on their desks. Rest period lasts about ten minutes. In some schools, the teacher reads the children a story during this time.

Rest period may be followed by another academic period in a subject area which was not covered earlier in the day. In addition, depending on the ethnic background of the children, the reading, writing, and speaking of Malay may be taught as a second language, since beginning with the 1970 academic year all primary schools were required to conduct standard one (first grade) in Malay. Each subsequent year the government planned to have sufficient texts and other materials in the national language in order to require the next succeeding grade to be completely converted to instruction in Malay.

After the academic work, which again takes thirty to forty-five minutes, there is an arts and crafts period. This may take several forms, but the most common activities are painting with watercolors or tempera, working with plasticene, doing collage work, using cut-and-paste books and coloring books, and doing free drawing. In painting the children may be free to paint what they like, or they may be assigned a subject.

In collage work, all children are given the same equipment and an assigned project—for example, to fill in an already drawn outline with bits of paper or seeds. The teacher places a bowl or basket of the collage materials in the center of each table. The children may have to provide their own glue and scissors, or the teacher may place several jars of glue and pairs of scissors for the children to share.

For work with plasticene, each child is given a lump of plasticene and a board on which to work. There may be an assigned project, or the children may make what they like. In one period observed, the children were asked to make zoo animals, having been taught to distinguish these from domestic animals during several of the periods devoted to training memory and observation skills. The children made a variety of clearly recognizable animals, such as giraffes, monkeys, bears, lions, and snakes.

Cut-and-paste books are very common. These are printed paper booklets in which there are both pages that are white with black line drawings and pages that have multicolored pictures. The colored pictures match various parts of the line drawing on the preceding or following page. The colored pieces must be cut out and then pasted in the correct place on the line drawing. Some have numbers on each piece to be cut and a matching number printed in the space in which that piece goes. These books are sequential and gradually increase the difficulty of the cutting task, the matching task, and the concepts which the pictures portray. Some of the booklets are very small, only about 3 by 4 inches; others are about 7 by 10 inches. Different publishers put out different series covering topics with various degrees of complexity. Each booklet and each picture have a title which is usually written in both English and Chinese.

Coloring books in Malaysian preschools are similar in many respects to the cut-and-paste books. Pictures are numbered and are of increasing difficulty in terms of the spaces to be colored, the number of colors to be used, the degree of color discrimination required, and the level of concept portrayed. These books are designed so that the cover, which has small multicolored versions of all the line drawings inside, can be placed either next to or above each drawing to be completed. The children are to match the colors in the small pictures when they fill in the lines in the coloring book.

Generally, the entire class does the same kind of work during the art period, and several different activities are not provided at the same time. However, in some cases there may be two activities during this period, the equipment for one put away before the next is undertaken. Usually, the children are permitted to converse quietly while they work, and the teacher walks among the desks observing, assisting when asked, and chatting with various children. This period lasts thirty to forty-five minutes. At the end the children clean up and put their things away. If there is a single assigned project, in some schools the children may engage in quiet indoor free play after they finish.

In some schools there may also be a brief music period devoted mostly to singing American and British children's songs. This usually lasts ten or fifteen minutes and may occur at any point during the day. A piano and a record player are the usual accompaniments.

At the end of the school day, about noon, the children either line up or stand behind their chairs for a prayer and an exchange of formal good-byes. Then they are dismissed.

RESEARCH AND FUTURE DIRECTIONS

In September 1973, a six-day national conference on the planning of early childhood education was held in Kuala Lumpur.[2] Participants raised a number of issues regarding the role of early education in compensating for socioeconomic disadvantage and in reducing dropout rates, especially among the rural poor. Working papers were presented on early education in Malaysia, the development of assessment procedures for Malaysian children, and ongoing research in family socialization. There was also concern for providing curricula to meet the different social and cultural backgrounds of the children.

Preschools reach a very small proportion of the children in Malaysia. Compulsory primary education is a continuing goal. Although there is some pressure to lower the entry age from six to five years, the shortage of primary teachers will hinder such a development. Given the discussions at the 1973 Seminar on Early Childhood Education, it appears that compensatory preschool education will continue to expand under governmental sponsorship. However, early schooling will remain in the private sector in the near future.

Educational research and evaluation are still in an early stage, and their expansion is hindered by scarce financial resources.[3] However, there is an active research community centered in the institutions of higher learning. At the 1973 seminar, research papers were presented on a number of topics, including the assessment of school readiness, child-rearing practices among the Malay, Chinese, and Indian groups, and the relationship between socioeconomic background and school success.

NOTES

1   *Area Handbook for Malaysia*, U.S.Government Printing Office, Washington, D.C., 1970, p. viii.

2   Ministry of Education (Malaysia) and Bernard Van Leer Foundation (the Netherlands), *Seminar Pendidikan Kanak-Kanak Peringkat Awal* ("Seminar on Early Childhood Education"), September 10–15, 1973, Dewan Bahasa dan Pustaka, Kuala Lumpur, Malaysia.

3   *Bulletin of the UNESCO Regional Office for Education in Asia,* no. 14, pp. 112–113, Bangkok, Thailand, June 1973.

CHAPTER 7

THAILAND

Thailand is an agricultural nation with approximately 80 percent of its 35 million people engaged in the farming of rice or crops of other types. Bangkok, the seat of the king and the government bureaucracy, dominates the countryside and is the only real city in a Western sense. Although several ethnic groups coexist within the country's geographical boundaries, notably Thai Islam, Chinese, Thai Malay, and Vietnamese, the country is relatively culturally homogeneous. Elements of this homogeneous culture include a common Thai language, an agricultural lifestyle based on wet-rice farming, a Theravada Buddhist world view, and shared concepts of status and roles attached to religious positions, civil service, rank, age, and wealth.

Historically, two lines of educational tradition, Buddhist classical and Western, have developed and are reflected in the contemporary educational system. Classical education—the study of Buddhist theology, literature, and other writings—has existed since 1274. In early days parents sent their male children to serve at the temples (*Wat*) and to receive instruction in writing, reading, mathematics, and religion. Typically, classical education was available for families who could afford the loss of labor incurred by sons leaving the family home. The Thai royalty supported and encouraged religious education, for they believed such learning contributed to spiritual and moral development and hence benefited the country.

In the seventeenth century, the classical educational system began to be influenced by contact with Western education. The Thai kings sent ambassadors and students to study in Europe. In exchange Thailand received ambassadors and missionaries from several Western European

NOTE: The research assistance of Ann Zavitkovsky in the preparation of this chapter is acknowledged.

countries. In 1871, government-supported schools were established to educate princes and to train the aristocracy for civil service positions. This form of education was secular and reflected English and French influence. In 1898, the Royal government attempted to model the Thai system on that of England. British influence is still found today in the persistence of the examination system, which determines promotion, allocation to vocational or academic secondary education, and access to the occupational structure in contemporary Thailand.

Although elements of classical and Western thought are found in the present educational system, the modern system inaugurated in 1921 by King Chulalongkorn (1868–1910) reflected new social, political, and economic demands on small Asian countries during the period. The King recognized the great need for the Thai government to demonstrate its ability to undertake administrative responsibilities, so that Thailand would not become dominated by Britain and France like its neighbors. Hence, the modern system of primary education was first devised on an immediate basis to train adults for staff positions in the administrative bureaucracy and, on a long-range basis, to help prepare children to be citizens of a nation that was becoming increasingly modernized. Thailand's development as an independent, modern, and strong nation was a primary goal.

In 1921, the Compulsory Education Act decreed that every child between ages seven and fourteen would be entitled to four years of free public education. As with other developing countries, provision of compulsory primary education was most highly developed in Bangkok, the capital, and less effective in the rural areas. Lack of facilities, supplies, and trained teachers limited expansion in the rural areas, where the incentive for primary education was small, since education was useful mainly to those aspiring to civil service positions. Parental attitudes in rural areas have been changing favorably toward education as a vehicle for social betterment whereby the children leave agricultural work and are trained for white-collar jobs. By about 1960, virtually all children, even those in the countryside, attended four years of primary school. In 1960, compulsory education was extended to seven years, and secondary education was modified to provide students with a background in technology necessary to meet the country's increased scientific and commercial needs. However, it has not been possible to enforce the law completely throughout the country, especially in the rural areas.

Thai law provides for seven years of compulsory education. The first four years in Thai schools are called the junior grades (ages seven to ten), followed by three years of senior grades (ages eleven to thirteen). In addition to reading and writing, the curriculum includes nature study, history, geography, mathematics, hygiene, and moral training. Religion and morality classes are compulsory at all levels of schooling, reflecting the traditional belief that an important function of schooling is to teach students to be model Thais. Secondary education is divided into academic and vocational streams lasting five to six years. Higher education usually lasts four years. Finally, preschool education is available to a limited number of children from ages three-and-a-half to six.

The cultural and religious background of the Thais influences their attitudes toward schooling in general and early schooling in particular. The philosophy of Theravada Buddhism emphasizes the primacy of individual action in the context of strong community support. It is believed that a child comes into the world already formed to some degree by his own accumulated merit. Each individual is thought to be solely responsible for working out his own destiny through cycles of birth and rebirth. The stress on individuality legitimizes the pursuit of self-concern and encourages relationships based on reciprocity.

Experiences in early childhood are subtly but profoundly influenced by this ethos and have a deep psychological impact. The parent-child relationship is in large degree contractual; both parent and child are conceptualized as being separate, linked by mutual cooperation. The parent raises the child while he is young, dependent, and helpless, and the child in turn takes care of the parent when the parent grows old. Thai families are noted for their closeness and stability. Deference to and dependence on authority throughout adult life is a Thai characteristic.

These factors are conducive to favorable attitudes about sending children out of the home to school. First, schools are regarded as an extension of the King himself and in this respect share in his prestige. Second, the firmness of the parent-child contract allows parents to feel relaxed about separation, as long as it is not seen as threatening to the contract. In fact, sending a child to school has definite advantages, in terms of the child's later ability to take care of the parent, because a better education will help the child secure a better job. Sending a child away to school during the day is a rather minor separation in view of the Thai tradition of sending a child away from his family altogether to live with other relatives or siblings. In the countryside, the preschool child is often in the care of grandparents while the mother works in the fields.

The Bangkok Institute for Child Study has conducted a series of studies on the relationship of child-rearing practices to children's school achievement and adjustment.[1] The findings of these studies conducted in different villages indicate a continuity in the values of the home and the school. Children are taught great respect for authority and for wisdom which accrues with age and are expected to respect teachers and those in positions of authority. Thai researchers conclude that there appears to be little "cultural discontinuity" experienced by the child in the transition from home to school.

EARLY SCHOOLING IN THAILAND

Thailand's first constitution, written in 1932, called for the establishment of kindergartens to prepare children for the first grade. However, it was not until 1940, in response to the high rate of failure during primary years, that the government began actively to support and supervise preschool education. A model government kindergarten, called *Laor-Utit*, using the methods of Froebel and Montessori, was started in 1940. A kindergarten teacher training center was also started with a workshop for the production of materials. This early beginning gave impetus to research into the "play-way" method, in which children learned practical words through actions, songs, and games. This method was also introduced in the primary grades. The movement also educated parents to understand the importance of individuality and adaptive intelligence over that of academic and memory training.[2] Since then, the Ministry of Education has undertaken several experiments to improve and extend preschool opportunities as a means of compensating for inadequate training prior to school entry at age seven.

Although the government has provided some support for preschools, financial resources have been limited. In Thailand as in many developing countries, funds for expansion of preschools are limited because of the more pressing need to provide basic education for older children and to provide the population with better health care programs, more adequate living conditions, and accelerated economic development.

In the last ten years, there has been a steady increase in enrollment in kindergartens (see Table 7.1).[3] In 1968, 4 percent of all children enrolled in government primary schools had attended kindergartens. Statistics recorded in 1970 indicated that 3 percent (approximately 103,613) of the preschool-age population (4 million) was enrolled in government-sponsored kindergartens. It was planned to expand the total enrollment to 139,000 children in 1974 and 189,000 in 1976. The statistics indicate that only a very small proportion of Thai children have preschool experience.

TABLE 7.1 KINDERGARTEN STATISTICS FOR 1964–1972

Year	Enrollment in Ministry of Education Programs	Total, All Types	Teachers	Number of Ministry of Education Schools
1964	13,673	65,627	669	NA*
1965	14,876	69,070	677	NA
1966	16,457	82,523	752	NA
1967	18,824	90,199	819	NA
1968	22,624	102,370	906	60
1972	42,977	154,127	1,543	72
				(1,325 classes)

* NA indicates not available.
SOURCE: The information for this table comes from two sources: Ministry of Education (Thailand), *Final Report, School and Teacher Census,* 1968; Ministry of Education (Thailand), *1972 Advance Report on Educational Statistics,* 1972. Enrollment figures are available for government-sponsored programs and private programs combined. However, the remaining statistics were collected on government programs only.

The teaching force for kindergartens increased steadily from 1964 to 1968. However, the student-teacher ratio in the kindergartens also increased during the same period from 20.4 to 1 in 1964 to 28 to 1 in 1970.[4]

The certificate in preschool education is obtained from a teacher-training college which is under the supervision of the Ministry of Education. Candidates must be secondary school graduates or hold a certificate in education or domestic science. The duration of training varies with respect to the previous educational background of the student. High school graduates study for four years and earn a secondary certificate. The training curriculum includes administration of pre-schools; child development; instructional approaches in social studies, science, music, and art; child health and nutrition; equipment and methods for fostering play; the skills needed for storytelling; child observation; and practice teaching. The salaries and working hours of preschool and primary teachers are similar. It is possible to change from one teaching level to another with Ministry approval.

Teachers are predominantly female (1,404), with a small minority male (139). Their training has improved in the last several years. Both the

Teacher Training Department and the Division of Special Education provide summer and in-service training in kindergarten programs. Table 7.2 presents statistics on the academic training of teachers in 1968 and 1972.

TABLE 7.2　PERCENTAGE OF TEACHERS AT DIFFERENT TRAINING LEVELS

Level	1968	1972
Bachelor's degree or higher	1.0	4.0
Diploma in education	17.4	51.0
Certification in education	45.0	35.0
Lower certificates or below	36.6	10.0

SOURCE: National Statistical Office and Ministry of Education (Thailand), *Final Report School and Teacher Census,* 1968; and *1972 Advance Report on Educational Statistics,* 1972.

There are basically five types of preschools in Thailand: private schools, government-operated kindergartens, demonstration schools attached to teacher-training schools, kindergartens attached to government primary schools, and rural Headstart-type centers. Private schools are organized by various individuals, groups, and religious organizations. These schools account for a majority of the preschool enrollment. Government-operated kindergartens are under the jurisdiction of the elementary education division of the Ministry of Education and are designed to be model or demonstration programs. The government has established seventy-four of these model kindergartens, three in Bangkok and one in each of the seventy-one provinces (*Changwat*) to encourage the expansion of other kindergartens in the provinces and to demonstrate good preschool practices. These schools vary in size, some having as many as 400 pupils, and they account for a very large minority of the total preschool enrollment. The Ministry provides teaching materials and playground equipment for these schools.

The goals of the government kindergartens, as stated by the department of elementary education, include:[5]

1　To prepare children to use eyes, hands, and tools in preparation for school
2　To bring up an observant, persevering, and patient man
3　To be self-reliant
4　To know manners and morals
5　To have healthy habits
6　To be faithful with the world—to be in society happily

The third type of preschool is the demonstration school attached to preprimary teacher training schools. These schools train preschool teachers, develop curricula suited to the needs of Thai children, and conduct research.

The first three types of preschools charge tuition, have fees for lunches, snacks, and supplies, and frequently require parents to provide uniforms. They enroll children between the ages of two and six.

The remaining two types of preschools are free, except for a minimal fee charged to cover the cost of lunches and snacks, and were established to educate the children of the urban and rural lower social classes. One type, supported by local municipal governments, in the form of one-year kindergartens attached to the government's primary schools. They were set up in response to pressure by parents who did not have access to private preschools because of financial reasons. The classes are for children ages five through six. After completing one year, the children are promoted to the first grade. These municipally sponsored kindergartens enroll about half as many children as the government model kindergartens. Although the methods and curricula used in all preschools are supposed to be similar, parental demand frequently forces these one-year programs to place an emphasis on formal academic preparation.

The final type of preschool program is the rural Headstart-type center. "Headstart" centers are set up near or are operated in conjunction with rural elementary schools in selected areas. Priority is given to those areas in which children speak a widely divergent dialect of the Thai language, where there are severe health problems, or where there is a governmental concern about political insurgency. The centers are run by teachers or teacher trainers who have been given a special course designed for this program by the department of teacher training. The objectives of these "Headstart" centers include:[6]

1 General objectives
   a To enhance the development of young children who come from lower cultural and educational families; to assist in their physical, emotional, mental and social growth
   b To enhance the readiness of children for the elementary level of education
   c To propagate modern methods of child rearing to the parents and people in the country
2 Specific objectives
   a To encourage good physical growth

b To enhance the readiness of children in reading, writing, and arithmetic

c To help children get along with their peer groups

d To enhance their manual skills through such things as painting or learning artistic subjects

e To teach them to move their muscles in the right way

f To encourage their creative ability

g To enhance their curiosity and to train them to have the courage to ask questions

h To encourage self-reliance

i To train them to have morality and discipline

All Thai preschools are subject to inspection and supervision by the Ministry of Education. Within the Ministry, kindergartens are under the jurisdiction of the Kindergarten Section, the Division of Special Education, and the Department of Elementary and Adult Education. There are three levels of kindergartens which enroll children from ages three to six: kindergarten grade one (three- to four-year-olds), grade two (five-year-olds), and preprimary (six-year-olds). Kindergartens must meet licensing requirements of building, equipment, safety, and sanitary standards. With the cooperation of preschool teachers and principals, the government has devised model syllabi which detail daily, weekly, and monthly programs. The syllabi are recommendations only and are not enforced. Although the time schedules in all schools are similar, curricula and teaching methods are not uniform.

Because of the limited numbers of schools, the Special Education Division has set up eligibility criteria for admission to the public kindergartens. First priority is given to orphans. Second and third priorities are given to children of single parents and to large families. Finally, priorities are given to children whose parents work in the Ministry of Education or in government-related areas.

The suggested curriculum developed by the Ministry of Education is divided into four time blocks, which include work period, music time, physical education, and the academic lesson. Work periods are designed to "encourage children to express ideas and to offer emotional release and sensory pleasures in the manipulation of blocks, fingerpaint, clay, tools, and other materials."[7] Music time includes singing games, folk dances, and classical Thai dances which are aimed at developing rhythmic body movement in the children. The physical program focuses on the development of large muscle coordination as well as developing "skills and attitudes towards sports and building better human relations."[8]

The final block, the academic lesson, is usually carried out informally. Lessons are put in the words of songs, rhymes, and stories which students can sing and easily remember. According to the official syllabus, "lessons are learned by repeating the teacher's words or listening to the story that the teacher is telling; by looking at picture books which the teacher reads aloud . . . by discussing experiences from excursions or field trips; and experimenting when playing or working."[9] Academic instruction is given in arithmetic, basic science, social studies (history, geography, ethics, and religion), Thai language, and creative arts.

Each school has the freedom to arrange its own daily schedule. Table 7.3 presents a schedule which is normally found in full-day kindergartens. Half-day schools have sessions from 8:45 A.M. to 12:30 P.M. and from 12:30 to 3:30 P.M.

TABLE 7.3 DAILY PRESCHOOL SCHEDULE

Time	Activity
8:45–9:00 A.M.	Health inspection; singing of national anthem and flag raising
9:00–10:00	Free activities
10:00–10:30	Snack and outdoor play
10:30–10:50	Hygiene; civics; moral education
10:50–11:20	Nature study; gardening; physical exercise, games
11:20–11:30	Toileting, bathing; preparation for lunch
11:30–12:00 noon	Lunch
12:00–2:00 P.M.	Nap
2:00–2:15	Bath
2:15–2:45	Stories; singing and music; language
2:45–3:00	Snack
3:00	Health inspection; departure

OBSERVATION OF THE SCHOOL DAY

The preschool day in Thailand formally begins at about 8:45 A.M. However, the grounds of most schools are open by about 7:00 A.M. for those children whose parents drop them off on the way to work. Children are brought to the schools by their parents, siblings, or servants or by bus if they attend the Ministry schools. The children engage in free play outdoors until the formal opening time. The range of outdoor equipment available depends on the school. Some have none, while others have several varieties of elaborate swings, slides, climbing equipment, sandboxes, and playhouses.

When it is time for school to open, a bell is rung, or the teacher claps her hands, and the children gather for a flag salute outside the school. In some schools the children remove their shoes before entering. They may go either into their classrooms or into an assembly hall, where they line up in rows for the exchange of morning greetings. Health (cleanliness) inspection and exercises may follow. The schedule of the remainder of the day is usually similar in almost all schools. The specific activities of any preschool may vary according to the philosophy of the school and teacher and may depend on the age of the children and the available equipment.

The first activity, lasting approximately an hour, may be devoted to either formal or informal academic instruction in the Thai language, arithmetic, social studies, nature studies, sensory training, reading, or writing. The activity may involve indoor free play with selected table-top toys and art materials. In some schools the younger children, ages two to four, engage in free-play-type activities while the older ones work on academic subjects.

Formal academic work is also given in schools for students of lower socioeconomic groups and in schools with a Roman Catholic affiliation. Instruction in these schools is carried out in much the same manner as in preschools of the Philippines. Middle- and upper-class Thai schools present formal work to children aged six and older. Printed workbooks are not generally available. For this reason, most of the work is done in homemade workbooks and by copying from the board. In most schools (through the university level) the language of instruction is Thai, the mother tongue. However, preschools often teach English as a second language.

The following English lesson exemplifies the less formal approach to academic work. The children sat on chairs in a semicircle, the teacher on a small chair facing the group. The lesson began with a recitation of Thai nursery rhymes accompanied by clapping. Then the teacher held up a series of pictures of animals, and the children chorused, in English, the name of each animal pictured. When the children did not know the name or were uncertain, the teacher prompted them, first in Thai and then English, and the children repeated the answer after her. The last picture was a kangaroo, and the teacher led the children in a Thai song, accompanied by gestures, about a kangaroo.

After holding up each card the teacher placed it on the floor, making a circle of the cards around her chair. She asked half of the children to stand and gave each one a different picture of an animal. Then, while the teacher led the rest of the group in singing "Bingo" in English, the children walked around the circle holding the pictures. At the end of the song each child had to place his picture next to the matching one on the floor. Once all had matched their animals, the teacher congratulated them, and the seated children applauded. Then the children handed their pictures to the seated children, and the game was repeated, this time singing "Loop-de-lou."

During periods of structured play, the teacher sets out various types of materials, one kind to a table—crayons and paper on one, beads and string on another, and plasticene and boards and tools, number toys, baskets of small plastic animals, blocks, or books on others. The children are free to move from table to table but must keep toys at the tables where they belong and must tidy up before moving to another table. During structured play the teacher also moves from table to table, working and talking with the children. If she sits at a table where children are stringing beads into chains of various lengths, she counts the beads on their chains, names the colors, and ties knots for necklaces and bracelets. If she sits at a table with crayons, she chats with the children about what they are drawing and hangs up completed pictures. Children who need supplies or assistance come to the teacher to make their requests. The teacher provides the requested assistance and then engages herself again with one of the groups. At the end of the play period, the teacher and children together collect all the equipment and put it away in cabinets.

At 10:00 A.M., in most schools, the children go to the lavatory and return for snack time. The lavatory routine varies according to the available facilities. In some schools the children go by themselves, while in others they are lined up to go as a group. The snack is provided by the school and includes a drink of either milk or fruit juice, fruit rolls, or crackers. The teacher or her assistant places the snacks on the tables. Before eating, the children, standing with hands folded, recite a prayer and bow. The teachers sit at the tables and eat with the children, chatting with them. In some schools, the children must return to their seats when they finish, after putting their utensils away. In others they may engage in free-play activities, either in the classroom or outdoors. If outdoor free play is the mode, frequently this interval is extended into a ten-minute recess.

There are then two activities lasting about half an hour each before lunch at 11:30. These might be academic subjects not covered earlier, again learned either formally or informally; a story period; art; music; outdoor play; or indoor play with table toys. Stories are usually told, not read; this is a common practice in most Asian preschools. The teacher may use her own visual aids as well as gestures to accompany the story. Frequently, the story is used as a point of departure for a group discussion which often is directed toward the development of memory and reasoning skills.

For example, in one school observed the teacher had made a cardboard box into a "story box." The box, which had been covered with paper and painted, had a rectangular hole cut in the bottom to make a window. On either side of the window was a pole with a long roll of paper attached at each end so that one could roll the paper up first on one pole and then on the other. The teacher had painted the story of the three pigs on the paper so that each scene represented another step in the story. She then set up the box under a tree in the grassy part of the play yard and seated the children on small mats and chairs on the grass.

The teacher showed them the first scene, a picture of the pigs, and asked them to count how many there were. The children counted on their fingers. Then the teacher told the story of the three pigs by turning the paper roll to a new scene as she reached each new part of the story. She pointed out various things in the picture as she told the story: the differences in the housing materials, the difference in the type of hide of the pigs and the wolf, the wolf's teeth, and so forth. When the story was over, all the children stood, placed their hands together, and bowed in the traditional Thai gesture for showing respect. Then the children sat down again, and the teacher asked them what a wolf and a pig "say." The children responded with the appropriate noises. The teacher then pointed to the last picture and asked the children what was happening. The children answered. She rolled the pictures back onto the original pole, stopping at about every other picture to ask the children what happened at that point in the story.

Art in the schools usually consists of painting, drawing, and clay (plasticene) or collage work. All children work at the same activity at the same time. Often there is an assigned topic related to one of the earlier activities of the day. If the children must move from one room to another for this activity, they are usually lined up in single file and quietly move to the new location.

At the end of the second of these periods, the children are again taken to the bathroom, and the teachers check that all the children wash their hands properly before lunch. The school provides the children with a hot lunch. The children may be served by the teacher or assistants, or they may line up to go to the kitchen for their trays, which are carried back to the classroom. Eating utensils for children in Thailand are usually metal tablespoons and sometimes large forks. Knives are never provided, as sharp instruments are considered too dangerous for young children. In most schools the group is led in a prayer before eating. In some schools the teachers eat with the children; in others they eat while the children nap. In either case, they do sit with the children and converse with them as they eat. If available, second and third helpings are provided to those children who request them. Each child puts her things away when she is finished.

Lunch is usually followed by a "bath" and then a nap. The children remove all their clothes, placing them on a chair or rack. In schools with adequate lavatory facilities, the children go to the bathroom and brush their teeth, use the toilet, and splash themselves with water, either from the taps or from long troughs. In schools located on a canal, the children jump into the canal for their bath. In schools without sufficient water or lavatory facilities, the children remove only their outer clothes and, dressed in their underwear (undershirts for boys, underpants for girls), splash water on their faces, arms, and legs.

After bathing, the children return to their classrooms, where they dry themselves with their towels and dust themselves with talcum powder. In some schools the children nap in pajamas brought from their homes. In these schools the children dress themselves with the help of teachers and assistants. In other schools the children sleep in their underwear or clothes. In all schools the children bring their own quilts, mats, sheets, or light blankets and pillows, which are placed on the floor or on cots or beds. In some schools the children sleep in a special room; in others they sleep in a part of the classroom.

Before napping, the children are led in a prayer and are then told to lie quietly on their mats or beds. In many schools the children, up to age seven, bring baby bottles filled with milk or juice, and the teachers pass these out to their owners, who suck them as they lie quietly. As in the Japanese day care programs, some teachers sit between two children and pat and rub them gently until they are quiet and relaxed enough to sleep. The teachers may also supervise from a distance, making sure that all children are quiet by giving disapproving looks to the restless ones. The nap begins about 12:30 or 1:00 P.M. and lasts until 1:30 or 2:00 P.M.

Following the nap, the children again bathe, powder themselves, and dress. After the children have a snack, schools without formal academic programs conduct a period of art, music, organized outdoor games, or outdoor free play. This period lasts until the end of the day, when the children are picked up. In formal academic schools, the afternoon is devoted to subjects not covered in the morning and to a "review and revision" time, during which the day's work is corrected. This practice has in part been derived from the temple system of education, in which the morning's work is corrected and memorized before lunch and is then recited correctly in the afternoon. Much of Thai education still relies heavily on drill, recitation, copying, and repetition. This emphasis is supported not only by tradition but also by parental expectations, the examination system, and the lack of equipment and materials, including books.

The school day ends at varying times, generally between 2:00 and 3:00 in the afternoon.

RESEARCH AND FUTURE DIRECTIONS

The Bangkok Institute for Child Study (formerly the International Institute for Child Study) was created in August 1955 by UNESCO and the Thai government. The institute was formed (1) to carry out cross-cultural research on child development, (2) to provide training of researchers from Thailand and other countries in methodology, child development, and guidance, and (3) to disseminate research findings about the education and guidance of children in school and home settings. In January 1963, the institute became a national center assisted by UNESCO's Technical Assistance Program and now concentrates its research activities in Thailand.

The institute was established at the College of Education, which has since become a new university called Srinakarintarawirote. The institute is a department of the university and plans to change its name to the Research Institute for Behavioral Sciences. Students take part in a two-year graduate training program leading to the master's degree in education, developmental psychology, educational psychology, experimental psychology, and social psychology. Intensive research experience in the institute's projects is emphasized.

The institute's research activities can be divided into two broad areas. In the area of basic research, a number of studies have focused on the socialization of Thai children in different regions of the country. Although the purpose of these studies has been to identify factors in the home, school, and community which may affect the child's adjustment to the school situation, the studies also provide a rich ethnography of Thai village culture and society, including physical setting, social organization, economic systems, kinship and family patterns, beliefs, values, and religious practices. Investigations have also covered a wide range of child-rearing variables, such as nursing and weaning, toilet training, independence training, sex-role identification, and development of social values. As indicated earlier, studies conducted in three villages indicate that in general Thai children enter the school situation easily. There is no conflict between the expectations and the standards of the school and the family. The child's early socialization experiences have taught him to accept parental and adult authority and have inculcated high respect for the teacher. The goal of both institutions is the development of good Thai citizens. A series of dissertations written by institute students has dealt with the development of learning processes in Thai children, especially in relation to the teaching of reading. As in other Asian countries, test construction to measure the intellectual development, the verbal and mathematics skills, and the interests of children has also been a focus of research activity.

The second broad area of the institute's research has focused increasingly on educational problems related to primary-age children. Present research activities include participation in the studies of the International Association for the Evaluation of Educational Achievement (IEA). Another study is directed toward understanding the problems a child experiences in reading Thai so that innovative methods and techniques for teaching reading and producing Thai reading textbooks may be developed. A long-term evaluation of the elementary school curriculum is being conducted, including a study of how achievement in academic subjects relates to self-concept, concept formation, need for achievement, self-confidence, and conscience. Another current study is being conducted on teaching science and mathematics concepts to seven- and eight-year-old children based on Piagetian theory.

In the field of child development and early education, the Bangkok Institute is one of the major research agencies in Asia. However, its research reflects a concern with the problems of primary education. No study to date has focused on questions of preprimary education in Thailand. In light of the need for decision-oriented educational research, the institute will continue to play an important role in the study of educational problems at the primary level. Its role in preschool education is less clear.

Kindergartens are now limited to only a small proportion of the preschool-age group. In its Third Five-Year Plan, the Special Education Division of the Ministry of Education outlined its goals for the period 1972–1976.[10] Plans included raising standards in public kindergartens, opening new schools in areas outside the capital city, providing new buildings to permit increases in enrollment, maintaining the pupil-teacher ratio of 30 to 1, and providing in-service training for kindergarten teachers. The government also intends to expand preschools in areas where the Thai language is not used. The Ministry of Education has asked temples in rural areas to provide preschool education. Presently, except for the few government kindergartens, preschools are accessible mainly to children of middle-class families. However, as the Thai economy expands, there will be increased emphasis on providing preschool places for children of working mothers.

NOTES

1 M. L. M. Jumsai, *Compulsory Education in Thailand,* UNESCO, Paris, 1951, p. 67.

2 Bangkok Institute for Child Study, *Summaries of Three Studies Concerning the Socialization of Children* Bangkok, 1967; Chancha Suvannathat, Niyom Kamnuanmasok, and Ladtongbai Bhuapirom, *Summaries of the Study of Social Influences on the Development of Thai Children in the Villages of Ban Pranmuen and U-Meng,* Bangkok Institute for Child Study, Bangkok, 1971.

3 The statistics used in this discussion are from the National Statistical Office and Ministry of Education, *Final Report, School and Teacher Census,* Bangkok, 1968, and *1972 Advance Report on Educational Statistics,* Bangkok, 1972.

4 Ibid.

5 Department of Elementary Education, Ministry of Education, *The Courses of Study for First Year Kindergarten Children,* Government of Thailand, Bangkok, no date.

6 Saiyut Champathong, *Program for Training Children before Normal School Attendance,* Ministry of Education, Department of Teacher Training, Government of Thailand, Bangkok, no date, p. 1.

7 *The Development of the Kindergarten School in Thailand,* Supervisory Unit, Department of General Education, Ministry of Education, Bangkok, no date, p. 9.

8 Ibid., p. 10.

9 Ibid., p. 11.

10 Ibid., pp. 13–14.

CHAPTER 8

INDIA

India is a vast country containing a population which is culturally and linguistically heterogeneous. Until becoming a British Crown Colony, India had little political unity. Though the northern areas were sometimes united under an empire, the south was composed of separate kingdoms.

The British first established trading centers on the subcontinent during the eighteenth century (1757–1857). By the beginning of the nineteenth century, they exercised political and economic control over virtually the entire country. A movement for national independence began in the late nineteenth century and gained momentum in the twentieth under the leadership of Mahatma Gandhi. In 1947, India achieved its national independence.

India today is the second most populous country in the world and accounts for approximately one-seventh of the world's population. The problems facing India include social and regional integration and economic development. When viewed within this context, the challenge of educational planning at all levels becomes exceedingly complex.[1]

While education was still under British domination, responsibility for it was transferred to the Indian ministers in 1921, and provincial autonomy was granted in 1937.[2] In the years 1946–47 a major expansion of the educational system took place based on the commitment to education as a means of social reform which evolved during the independence movement.[3] Since declaring its independence, India has made massive strides toward the goal of equal educational opportunity. However, because of cultural and linguistic differences and the fact that 80 percent of the population is rural, the task remains a difficult one.

Authority and responsibility for providing education has been dele-

gated to the states. Thus thirty states and union territories are responsible for establishing schools, curricula and texts, examinations, and
innovations to fit local conditions. The national constitution states that
free and compulsory primary education shall be provided for all children
up to the age of nine. In all union territories and in nine states, education
is free for children through the age of seventeen. However, the availability of free education varies among the states. In 1973, the national
average of attendance for compulsory education was estimated at 68
percent.[4]

The definitions of primary and secondary schooling vary according
to state, though the system in general reflects British influence. Lower
primary schools serve children between the ages of seven and eleven;
senior primary schools are for children from eleven to fourteen; there are
non–college preparatory secondary schools for fourteen- to seventeen-
year-olds; and college preparatory higher secondary schools serve four-
teen- to eighteen-year-olds. In 1965, roughly 59 percent of the age-group
population were enrolled in primary school; 15 percent of the age-group
population were enrolled in middle and secondary schools. Approximately 3 percent of the age group were enrolled in institutions of higher
education.[5]

Classes in Indian primary schools are large (the teacher-pupil ratio is
about 1 to 30), and the curriculum is focused on basic skills. The
language of instruction is the predominant language of the state, which
may or may not be the children's mother tongue. Fourteen state
languages out of the more than 105 Indian languages are used for
instruction. If the instructional language used is not Hindi, the national
language, children must learn it as well as English. Thus, Indian children
must often learn to read and write a minimum of two and sometimes
four languages, including two or more alphabet systems.

Before British domination, education in India took place in religious
institutions, first under the Brahmans and then under the Muslims. Both
groups had schools ranging from the equivalents of primary through
university levels. After British domination, education remained largely
voluntary until the mid-nineteenth century, when missionary groups and
private enterprises provided English-based education in those areas
under British control. In 1835, the British governor of India declared that
it was the responsibility of the British government to provide education
for the Indian people. From this time on, the British began re-creating an
English educational system in India. Secondary schools for the sons of
the elite were encouraged with the hope of training loyal subjects and
future civil servants.

The traditional elite literary British educational system, which was described earlier (see Chapter 4), meshed well with Indian educational theories, philosophies, and practices. Indian theory regarded education as a necessity for and prerogative of the elite social classes. Traditional religious thought required that young men of the higher social classes or castes devote their youth (ages eight to twenty) to the study of religious literature. In theory, they were to be introduced ceremonially to the alphabet at the age of five and would begin their mastery of basic skills at home. They were then to live with and serve their teachers in exchange for their education. In actual practice, children were taught at home by a tutor or in groups at the home of a village teacher. The curriculum was oriented toward teaching the basic skills. Stories taken from the great religious, historical, and philosophical epics provided the basis for instruction. The usual age of admission to study was between four and six years, though it was common practice for children of many ages to study together. The course of study lasted about four years unless there was a remarkably well-educated or gifted teacher available.

The establishment of universal, compulsory education was one of the major platforms of the Indian independence movement. The great Indian leader, Mahatma Gandhi, emphasized rural, social, political, and moral reconstruction by means of basic education (*Nai Talim*). He proposed and actively worked for an educational system which included and emphasized a preschool level. According to Gandhi, prebasic education (the first stage in basic education) was the education of children under seven for the development of all their faculties, conducted by school teachers in the schools, in the home, and in the village in cooperation with the parents and the community. This education was aimed at the whole child—the physical, mental, moral, cultural, and spiritual aspects of human development. As practiced in rural areas, prebasic education had two important social objectives. First, it would prepare citizens to fit a new communal society. Second, it would become the basis of and would produce social, political, and economic reforms. In fact, all reforms were seen to have their origins in prebasic education.

Prebasic education was divided into four stages in accordance with the child's age. The first stage (until birth) is actually adult education. The parents are trained in child-rearing practices, infant care, health, and nutrition. The second stage (birth to 2½) focuses on the child's physical health and on the provision of custodial care. At 2½ years (the junior level), the child can leave his mother for two to three hours per day to attend classes. At this level, the child engages in free play and exploration. The role of the teacher is to prepare an environment that is exciting to the children so that they are motivated to explore and develop their knowledge of the world. In doing so they will use language to express themselves. At ages four through seven (the senior level), the child is socialized to develop positive attitudes toward work and its dignity. The child begins to engage in useful and meaningful activities such as cleaning the classroom and taking responsibility for her needs. Work and play are integrated. The activities are related to the importance of the industrial and economic development of India, based on a society in which the distinction between the intellectual and the working class would not be great. Further development of language and artistic goals including art, music, singing, and rhythm is pursued along with nondenominational community worship. At age six, readiness activities are used to prepare the child for basic education.

Two other principles are essential to Gandhi's conception of education. Gandhi conceived the role of the teacher as one of close collaboration with the home, community, and the parents. In this role, teachers maintain contact with parents through home visits and parent meetings. Gandhi believed that materials and equipment utilized in instruction should be related to the life and traditions of the local people and in this way unite the home and school. Materials must be inexpensive and should originate from the experience and world of the child.

EARLY SCHOOLING IN INDIA

Preschool education in India began during the last quarter of the nineteenth century when various private and missionary schools were formed to serve children of the higher social classes in the urban areas of Delhi, Madras, Calcutta, and Bombay. They began to include either Froebelian kindergartens or British nursery and infant departments in their educational programs. Children were prepared for entrance into the primary and secondary departments of the same schools. Montessori preschools, also emphasizing preparation for primary school, were introduced around 1920, either as separate establishments or attached to primary schools. The arrival of Dr. Montessori in India in 1939 and her extended stay greatly influenced the nature of preschool education.[6] Many Indian people still associate preschools with the Montessori method. The Montessori schools were adapted by various social and educational reformers to be consistent with the needs of Indian life, specifically the education of the children of lower castes and those living in rural areas. The Montessori method was also incorporated to some extent in the Gandhian notion of prebasic education.[7]

Prior to independence in 1947, preschool education was provided solely by private schools. During preindependence planning, in 1944, the Central Advisory Board of Education (CABE) on Post-War Educational Development in India (the Sargent Report) recommended that the provision of preprimary education be an essential part of the educational system. However, growth of the preschool did not begin until the fifties.[8]

In 1953, the national government's Central Social Welfare Board expressed concern regarding the education of rural and poor children by establishing a nationally sponsored system of centers called *Balwadis*. Under the Third Five-Year Plan (1960–1965), training centers for Balwadi personnel, the *Balsevikas*, were established. A number of pilot projects for providing integrated child welfare services were also initiated during this period.

In the last decade, although a number of national committees have addressed themselves to the problems of providing services to India's children, the priority of the Indian government continues to be the achievement of universal primary schooling. Limited resources prevent the expansion of preschool programs and explain the lack of trained personnel, facilities, and equipment. However, professional interest in early child care and education is strong and continues to provide the impetus for the expansion of services for children.

In 1969, preschool-age children represented 16.5 percent of the population of India. Most of these children live in rural areas.[9] In describing the status of the preschool child (ages two to six), Mina Swaminathan wrote: "There are about 70 million children between 2 and 6 in India, and their first problem is to survive."[10] Forty percent of all deaths in India occur among children below five years of age. Swaminathan estimates that 75 percent of the child population can be classified as "not healthy," owing to illness originating from widespread malnutrition and related disorders. Within this context, the question has been raised as to whether an educational program for young children is the matter of greatest importance in India.

Many Indian preschool educators have dealt with this question in their writings.[11] They often stress the critical importance of the first six years of life, in terms of both the biological and the psychological development of the child. The studies conducted by Benjamin Bloom are commonly referred to in addition to physiological studies of the brain. This period is viewed as critical, since poor health, growth, and development cannot easily be reversed by later remediation.

As in other Asian countries, preschool education is associated with the problem of failure in the primary schools. Hence, preschools have a compensatory origin much like those in America. It is hoped that through preschools, children from poor families can be prepared emotionally and intellectually for the primary school experience. Preschool education is viewed as critical in a country where adult illiteracy is prevalent and where large numbers of children come from families who are unacquainted with the school system and its value.

In addition to its compensatory function, the preschool in India is seen to serve a social protection function. In urban areas, maternal employment is increasing, and the Indian extended family is disappearing. Hence, many young children are either left to care for themselves or remain under the supervision of siblings. The preschool is especially important for these children as a supplement to the home and mothering.

Finally, the purpose of preschool education is related to the need for social reform and intellectual preparation in a society that is becoming more technological. In many rural settings, the preschools are believed to be the basis for a program of social change affecting children, families, and communities.[12] This idea is consistent with Gandhi's notion of prebasic education. Other early educators have portrayed the ideal preschool as presenting "a kind of stimulus-induced preparedness as a foundation for later development in a technologically-based society."[13] The importance of "preparedness" becomes even more vital to children living in the rural areas where the child's environment is lacking in "technological stimuli" such as mechanical and electrical devices. An additional problem is that cognitive modes developed in rural environments may interfere with school learning and the acquisition of attitudes and values to fit a developing country.

In summary, the main arguments for the provision of preschool education in India are the belief that the first six years of life are the most critical years in the development of the child, the compensatory effects of the program in terms of preventing later failure, the social protection function of the preschools, the preparation of the child for a modern technological society, and the use of preschools as part of a program of social reform.

Organization of Early Schooling

Indian preschools fall into a wide range of categories. Among these are Montessori schools, prebasic nursery schools, the laboratory schools, the Balwadis, and a variety of social welfare programs. In the 1880s, kindergartens were established by the missionaries and were adapted to Indian conditions, emerging as Balwadis ("children's orchards") or as *Bal-Mandirs* and *Sishu-Vihars* ("houses of children"). Maria Montessori's visit in 1939 influenced the formation of preschools using the Montessori method. The Indian version of the Montessori method became extremely popular owing to a network of training institutes established after Montessori's visit. Since the late fifties, laboratory nursery schools associated with various Indian universities have been established, based on American and British models of progressive child development approaches.

Although preschools are mainly in the private and voluntary sector, the Balwadi program represents governmental involvement in the comprehensive care of children from low socioeconomic backgrounds. In addition to the Balwadi programs, the Central Social Welfare Board sponsors a number of other programs. Voluntary social welfare organizations are given grants to promote Balwadis in both urban and rural areas. The Welfare Extension Project focuses on teaching mothers and providing their children with nutrition, health, education, and welfare services. The Coordinated Welfare Extension Project conducts similar programs. The Family Welfare Projects in the Fourth Plan emphasize the education of mothers in home crafts, child care, and child welfare. This program also offers integrated services to children in rural areas.

In general, different programs are directed at the preschool child, providing a number of different services. For example, the Applied Nutrition Program has the main purpose of providing a nutritional feeding program for the child. The program also provides for parent education, nutritional education in the community, and the training of local women. Because of the diversity of these programs, it is difficult to provide a neat picture of services from which individual children benefit. Table 8.1 provides a summary of the types of programs in existence and their sponsoring agencies.

In a country as large as India with a predominantly rural population and problems of economic survival, it is difficult to collect statistical data, especially for noncompulsory, predominantly private programs like preschools. Even in urban areas, a large number of private preschools go unreported. Furthermore, figures often do not include classes attached to primary units. Table 8.2 provides an overview of preschool education in India based on available information. This information should be considered as minimum estimates since the original surveys were not considered to be complete.

As Table 8.2 indicates, the rate of increase in the number of schools and students has been large. However, the children represented by the statistics make up approximately 2.1 percent of the age group. As in

TABLE 8.1   SPONSORSHIP OF EARLY SCHOOLING PROGRAMS

Sponsor	Program
Private organizations and church bodies	Nurseries and kindergartens
Indian Council for Child Welfare and Central Social Welfare Board	Balwadis (urban and rural) Balsevika training
All-India Women's Conference, Guild of Service, Madras, Bharat Suwak Sumaj, All-Indian Balkan-Ji-Bari, Bal Niketan Sangh, Kishore-Dal, Nutan Bal Sikshan Sangh, Bombay, Children's Education Societies in Gujarat-Mysore/Delhi	Teacher training Day nurseries Preprimary schools Balwadis Child health centers
Montessori Association in India	Montessori schools
Education and community development departments in the states	Nursery schools Teacher training Prebasic schools
Labor and social welfare departments in the states	Crèches Maternity centers Day care centers Health centers
Other voluntary organizations and industrial sector	Day care Mobile crèches

SOURCE: Adapted from Indian Association for Preschool Education, *Systems of Preschool Education in India*, Rakesh Press, Delhi, no date, p. 105.

TABLE 8.2   PRESCHOOL STATISTICS

Year	Schools	Rate of Increase, %	Enrollment	Rate of Increase, %
1950–51	303		28,309	
1955–56	630	52	45,828	36
1960–61	1,909	66	121,122	62
1965–66	3,500	53	250,000	51

SOURCE: *Education in India* and *Education Commission Report, 1964–1966.*

other Asian countries, preschools in India remain the luxury of the rich and are primarily an urban phenomenon. In the rural and central city areas, the number of preschools is small. Also, although most of the

Indian population is agrarian and rural, the rate of increase of preschools in rural areas is strikingly slow. In 1950–51, 9 percent of the country's preschools were located in rural areas. Since that time, the annual rate of increase in rural preschools has been less than 15 percent.[14]

A more detailed picture of the variety of services available to children is presented in the report of the 1972 national committee on preschool education.[15] Programs were divided into education, nutrition, health, and welfare services. In 1970, educational services of different types provided by private preschools and Balwadis were estimated to reach 1 million children. Nutritional programs, which are run by the Department of Social Welfare, benefited 212,160 children. Under the programs of the Central Welfare Board, 1 million children were served. Statistics were not available on the number of children reached by maternal and child health services, but approximately 2 million preschool children are covered by one or more programs.

Both public and private institutions for the training of preschool teachers are available but limited. There are 100 preprimary teacher-training institutions throughout India, with wide variations in admission standards, courses of study, and purposes. The Balwadi program provides its own training course for the teacher, or Balsevika, who is a multipurpose worker in child health, nutrition, and welfare. National organizations such as the Indian Council for Child Welfare, the Central Social Welfare Board, and the Kasturba Memorial Trust also conduct training courses. Montessori training programs are private. However, the influence of the Montessori method is strong, and many institutions have been based on its precepts.

Since there are no certification requirements, training, salary, and working conditions vary for teachers. As in many other countries, teachers are not well paid and as professionals are given a low social status. There are no fixed pay scales or job security except in the government schools.

Although training programs vary according to the institution and the state, women in preparation for preschool teaching typically take one-year courses including studies in child psychology, child development, school organization and management, health and nutrition, history, teaching methods, child welfare, and parent and community education. Practice teaching is also required. Advanced training in preschool education is virtually nonexistent, although individuals may obtain M.S. and Ph.D. degrees in child development with a specialization in preschool education.

Starting in 1974, a demonstration training course was planned for teachers at the primary and preprimary levels, the first year of training concentrating on preprimary education.[16] At the end of the year, teachers may leave the program and teach in preschools. Students who remain the second year will then be trained for primary levels. This program has been aimed at broadening the training of primary teachers in the use of child-centered practices (i.e., individualization and the play-way method). The results of this experimental approach will be awaited with interest.

The lack of adequately trained personnel in the field of preschool education continues to be a matter for concern in India. Considering the vast number of preschool-age children, the expansion of preschool education necessitates a flexible approach to qualifications and training of the teachers. The Study Group on the Development of the Preschool Child recommended in its report the training of paraprofessionals as well as the part-time employment of educated women and students to serve in the preschools.[17]

OBSERVATIONS OF THE SCHOOL DAY

The Indian preschool generally opens between 8:30 and 9:00 A.M. The children are brought by parents, siblings, servants, busses, or taxis, or they come on their own. They normally engage in free play until the formal opening, which varies from school to school. In some schools a morning assembly is held with formal presentations, group singing, and a prayer. It is common in some schools for children to be lined up in rows outdoors for a morning greeting, a prayer, and group singing in a fashion similar to that in the Philippines. Or the children may simply stand and greet the teacher in the customary manner (hands folded together and head bowed). There are also schools without any formal opening ceremonies, where the children simply exchange greetings with the teacher individually as they arrive.

Following morning greetings the school day is generally divided into half-hour periods. The day ends at 1:00 or 1:30 P.M., with lunch generally at noon. The time schedule and activities of the schools vary according to the sponsorship and goals of the individual school. Table 8.3 presents a schedule of a day in a laboratory nursery school attached to a training institute. In contrast, the schedule of a private Montessori school is shown in Table 8.4. It is important to keep in mind these variations in schedules, goals, teachers, facilities, and students when reading the following descriptions of preschool programs.

TABLE 8.3   SCHEDULE OF A LABORATORY NURSERY SCHOOL

Time	Activity
8:30–9:00 A.M.	Arrival; health inspection; toilet; wash hands; help in arranging flowers; dusting; caring of pets; putting out movable equipment
9:00–9:45	Outdoor free play
9:45–10:00	Putting away equipment; toilet; wash hands
10:00–10:15	Snack
10:15–10:30	Rest
10:30–10:50	Stories and nursery rhymes with music and rhythmic activities
10:50–11:30	Indoor free play
11:30–12:00 noon	Putting away material
12:00	End of school

SOURCE: L. Prem Das, *Preschool Education in Delhi,* report of a survey carried out in 1962, Navin Press, Delhi, 1974, pp. 30–31.

TABLE 8.4   SCHEDULE OF A PRIVATE MONTESSORI SCHOOL

Time	Activity
8:30–9:00 A.M.	Prayer
9:00–9:30	Hindu reading
9:30–10:00	Arithmetic
10:00–10:30	Hindu writing
10:30–11:00	Break
11:00–11:30	English reading
11:30–12:00 noon	English writing
12:00–12:30 P.M.	Counting and action songs
12:30	End of school

SOURCE: L. Prem Das, *Preschool Education in Delhi,* report of a survey carried out in 1962, Navin Press, Delhi, 1974, p. 30.

Balwadis

Balwadis were originated in the early 1950s under the auspices of the Central Social Welfare Board and the Community Development Administration. Their purpose was to meet the needs of rural children. In 1973, approximately 13,500 Balwadis in rural and small urban areas provided services to 650,000 children.[18] Financing for these schools comes from the central government and is allocated through the Department of Social

Welfare. Local communities contribute a portion of the operating costs. Authority to operate programs is delegated to local agencies and to community people. Voluntary associations such as the Kasturba Gandhi National Trust have also set up many Balwadis. In some Balwadis, a small fee is charged, though most are free. The program emphasizes child health, nutrition, recreation, and social welfare services for the family. The educational component varies according to individual programs. In some cases, the Balwadi functions mainly as a nutritional feeding program.

Balwadis are open most of the year, and each serves twenty-five to fifty children (2½ to 6 years old) and is operated six days a week. Depending on local community needs, Balwadis are operated for either half days or whole days. A half-day Balwadi is open three to four hours a day, while whole-day Balwadis are adjusted to the working hours of the mother. The Central Welfare Board recommends that during the sowing and harvest seasons, the Balwadi should be open for the entire day to provide care for children whose parents work in the fields.

Balwadis are usually located in community facilities or temples. The Central Social Welfare Board recommends that a Balwadi include an assembly room, storeroom, kitchen, teachers' living room, drinking well, and toilet facilities. Murals and children's pictures are recommended as decorations. Playgrounds with a sandbox and wading pool are also suggested. It is understood that many villages will not be able to meet these guidelines, but they are encouraged to exercise initiative and imagination in creating a Balwadi to meet the local conditions. Since there is no official program, curricula and methods also vary greatly. Teachers in Balwadis are encouraged to select their own methods. In some schools, Montessori methods are applied to Indian materials. Children learn to cut mangos, grind seed into flour, and pour water.

The model Balwadi is visualized as providing an integrated program for meeting the total needs of the child. The program would offer health, nutrition, education, and recreation services. The objectives include:

ı To help the child in its physical growth by
  a Immunization against diseases such as diphtheria, whooping cough, typhoid, tuberculosis, small pox, etc.
  b Health checkup at the time of admission to the Balwadi
  c Follow-up with medical aid from the nearest health center
  d Provision of balanced meals or a supplementary nutritive diet in the Balwadi after studying the home conditions
  e Healthful recreation

2 To help the child in the development of senses—touch, taste, smell, sight, and sound

3 To help the child learn the act of social adjustment with a view to developing healthy relationships with other children and adults

4 To train the child to take care of himself and to encourage the formation of healthy habits

5 To develop the child's intellectual capacity and to give him opportunities to explore, investigate, and experiment within his environment

6 To give training in discipline, regularity, and concentration and to teach the child the beginning of language and numbers

7 To encourage manual dexterity through various equipment so as to enable the child to handle things around him

8 To provide day care for children of preschool age[19]

According to the Central Welfare Board, activity and freedom are the guiding principles of the Balwadi. There are, of course, variations in the implementation of all objectives. Variation is encouraged by the Central Welfare Board so that practices for rural preschool education can be designed to fit the needs of the community. A list of equipment and furniture is provided by the central board. However, Balwadis are encouraged to prepare materials with the assistance of the children and their families from resources available in the community.

The Balwadis are staffed by Balsevikas ("servants of the children"), who undergo a special training program after completing the middle-school examination. This training program emanated from a community development effort which was conceived as a means of providing support personnel in the fields of farming, health, and veterinary care. The Balsevika is expected to provide linkage services between the Balwadi and the family and between the Balwadi and other social agencies serving children. The Balsevika training course, which lasts six to ten months, includes health and nutrition, child psychology, prepri-mary education, and child welfare courses. The Indian Council for Child Welfare trains Balsevikas in eleven centers located in different states.

A typical half-day sequence of activities in a Balwadi is as follows:

1 Washing and bathing; physical inspection of teeth, nails, and body; and morning prayer and songs.

2 Outdoor play, garden work, walks, and care of pets. Extending the child's experiences in community life and agriculture is also encouraged as a means of providing the child with a knowledge of his environment. These activities will also increase his vocabulary, concepts, and social skills.

3 Handwork and art including drawing and painting.

4 Snacks.

5 Rest.

6 Learning of language and numbers and nature study.

7 Free play with educational and constructive toys.

8 Storytelling, music, dance, and rhythms.

A rigid timetable is not recommended. Activities are planned to suit the needs and desires of children.

Bettelheim visited an urban Balwadi in 1969. The "classrooms," located in long corridors ringing an auditorium at the balcony level of a community center, were formed by large movable bulletin boards placed at various intervals. The floors were concrete, as were the walls. There were a few fluorescent light fixtures spaced along the ceiling. Each classroom was equipped with a worn cotton rug, a few rough tables about one foot in height, and a blackboard partition. There were some paintings by the children or teachers on the walls. The equipment of the school, stored in a closet, consisted of broken slates, chalk, tempera paint, brushes, used paper such as the back of mimeographed papers and newspapers, some new paper, and metal drinking cups.

The children, ages four through five, were seated on the floor at two tables. The tables were placed at the edge of a rug which was facing an aisle about four feet in width. Approximately six children sat on either side of each table. At one end of the aisle was a blackboard, at the other a wall. Each child had a broken slate and a piece of chalk for starting a writing lesson. The teacher began by slowly writing a letter from the Hindi alphabet on the board and saying the letter's name and its sound. The children repeated after her in unison the name and the sound. Then the teacher drew a picture of a flower in a flower pot to the right of the letter. The children said the letter and then the word which names the picture. They then repeated the sound of the letter. The teacher slowly wrote another letter below the first. She demonstrated how to form each stroke while saying its name and its sound. The children repeated after her. Next she drew a picture of an object beginning with that letter. The children chorused the name and the letter several times at the teacher's direction.

She then took a damp cloth and, going from child to child, erased each slate with it. She went to the blackboard, where she pointed to each letter and repeated its name and sound. Then she erased them and wrote them again more carefully and asked the children to try to write the letters on their slates. As the children began, they called to the teacher to show their work or to ask for help. The teacher helped each child in turn. When requested, she erased a slate so that a child could try again. Although she inspected the work of all the children, she volunteered no criticism of mistakes, and only if a child asked for help did she intervene other than to offer praise. If a child asked for help, he was taken to the blackboard, where the teacher drew the first stroke of the letter. She then gave the chalk to the child and told him where to place the next stroke. If the child had difficulty, the teacher took the child's hand in hers and guided it to form the rest of the letter. Smiling, the child returned to his seat, and the teacher returned to answering the requests of the other children.

After a time, the teacher called for the group's attention and, pointing to the first letter on the board, asked the children what it was. The group chorused the name of the letter. She did this for each letter and then called on individual children. Each child called said the name and sound of the letter and the name of the object pictured. The teacher repeated what the child said, and the children chorused after her. About six children were asked to do this. When the lesson was over, the children helped the teacher collect the slates and chalk. The children were then lined up in single file to proceed outdoors for a period of play. Following the outdoor period the children visited the lavatory and had lunch, which was preceded by a prayer. In this Balwadi the children brought their own lunches. Those without lunches sat in silence while the others ate. The school served a powdered milk mixture to all children. Recess followed lunch, and then came a period of arts and crafts or further academic work until dismissal.

Laboratory Nursery Schools

Laboratory nursery schools are viewed as places where new methods and curricula are developed that will be used as models for other preschools. These schools are typically attached to university departments of child development, to colleges of home science, to institutes of education, or to preschool teacher-training institutions. These schools base their methods on the theories of Comenius, Pestalozzi, and Froebel and appear to be similar in philosophy and practice to the American progressive nursery school movement. For this reason, the laboratory schools have been accused of being guided by Western ideas. However, there has been a continuing effort to adapt these ideas to Indian conditions.

As outlined by Margaret Varma, the laboratory nursery school has four broad objectives: to help the student teachers understand human growth and development through observation, participation, and teaching; to provide an optimal environment for young children; to promote among parents greater understanding of child growth and development and child rearing; and to facilitate research studies in child development and psychology.[20]

In a laboratory nursery school which is a model program promoted by the Indian National Institute of Education, the following observation of the day's activities were made. Upon arrival at the school, children engaged in outdoor free play with various playground equipment. Because of hot temperatures during the summer, the outdoor play period lasts no more than half an hour. In winter, the children play outside for up to an hour, depending on the time they arrived. At the end of the free play the children were lined up in single file to go indoors.

Once in the classroom, the children had a short period of calisthenics accompanied by rhythmic counting and followed by a music period, in which the children moved in time to rhythms produced by the teacher's beating a drum or tambourine. During this time there might also be teacher-led singing and dramatic play with teacher and children pantomiming the events of the school day: getting up, washing, dressing, eating, brushing teeth, and going to school.

Following was a period of indoor play in which the teacher set various types of equipment at tables or in various parts of the room. This equipment might include blocks, seeds of various types and bowls for sorting them, crayons and paper, and scissors and magazines for cutting. The children moved from task to task while the teacher sat and worked with various groups and answered requests for help.

The indoor play period is sometimes followed by a teacher-led group discussion based on something that happened either on that day or on the day before. For example, if a child brings some flowers to school, the teacher may use the opportunity as a basis for a discussion about the various parts of a flower, analyzing the functions of each part, its color, and its smell.

The group may use this period to take a field trip to a local place of interest, such as a construction site, a shop, or a garden. The children will have a discussion about the trip on the following day.

In all Indian preschools, the children are lined up and taken to the lavatory before lunch. In most of the schools either the teacher, the servant, or both will crouch next to the lavatory entrance to help the children unbutton and button their clothing. The children's hands are inspected for cleanliness as they exit. The children rinse their hands, all using the same towel for drying. If they wish a drink at this time, they may also take one of the cups provided and get water from the tap. An adult usually flushes the toilets, generally by pouring water in each. The children are lined up as they leave the lavatory, and once the group is all together, they return to the classroom for lunch.

At the laboratory school observed, the children put placemats or napkins on the table, took out their lunches, and placed the food on the mats. After a brief prayer, they sat and ate. In some cases, the teacher may put a receptacle for trash in the center of each table. The children cleaned up their things when they finished eating.

In the schools in which recess follows lunch, the children play outdoors, watched by a servant, while the teachers congregate to eat their own lunches.[21] If rest follows lunch, the children may simply lie on a rug while looking at old magazines and chatting or listening to the teacher telling a story.

In the school observed, after the story, the children were led by the teacher in singing games. The singing period was followed by a period of outdoor organized games. They were lined up to move from one location to another. After the games, the group returned to the class-room for group singing and chanting of rhymes or for a teacher-led discussion. This was followed by a formal exchange of good-byes between teacher and class before dismissal.

Private Schools

Private preschools also vary widely in facilities, equipment, and staff services. Some are similar to the Balwadis, while others are modeled after the laboratory schools. Still others are elegant schools for the children of the upper classes. There are also Montessori schools, which range from accredited schools with all the necessary equipment and well-trained teachers to those with very little Montessori equipment and staffed by poorly trained or untrained teachers.

The language used in most private schools, except those catering to the upper classes, is generally the mother tongue of the children. Schools for the upper classes use English as the medium of instruction, as do the exclusive primary and secondary schools. Higher education is available in several Indian languages; however, in India, as elsewhere, opportuni-ties are greater in higher education if one is fluent in English.

The following activities were observed at an exclusive private preschool. The children were seated cross-legged on mats, as is customary in India, in two rows facing each other, ready to begin a lesson in number concepts. There were between twenty and thirty children in the class with one teacher per class. The teacher handed each child a cotton pull-string sack containing bottle caps and a page from a calendar, on the back of which numbers from one to six were written along the left edge. An equivalent number of circles, slightly larger in diameter than the bottle caps, had been drawn next to each number. After the children placed their paper on the mat in front of them, they were asked to put one bottle cap on each circle.

The teacher walked between the two rows of children, stopping in front of individuals and asking them to count the number of caps they had placed in each row. She demonstrated that they should use their finger to point to or touch each cap as they counted. If a child did not count correctly, the teacher took his finger in her hand and touched each top in the row as she counted. Then she asked the child to count the row. When the child did so, she asked him how many tops there were. Once she was assured that the children understood the numerical concepts up to six, she allowed them to make successive rows of seven, eight, and nine. The teacher went from child to child, questioning, helping, correcting, and praising each one. She returned several times to those who did not understand.

At an appointed time, the teacher asked the children to put their caps in the sacks and to place the sacks in a basket at the end of the row. She collected the papers from each child. Once all were reseated in the correct places, she asked the children to count with her. With the teacher leading, the group counted up to twenty in unison, clapping to the rhythm of the counting. Then the teacher asked them to stretch their arms out in front of them as they counted to ten, then over their heads as they counted again to ten. The teacher reminded the children to count with her, not after her, and as she walked between the two rows, she touched the hands of the children who were not clapping. Next they counted as far as they could. Then, still walking up and back between the two rows of children, the teacher led the group in chanting various nursery rhymes, such as "Little Miss Muffet" and "Pussy Cat, Pussy Cat."

Following the number lesson, the children were lined up in single file and marched in silence to the physical training area, where they participated in a modified variety of calisthenics in time to music on a record player. A special physical training teacher led the activities. After physical training, the children had art or crafts, a trip to the lavatory, outdoor free play, another trip to the lavatory, nursery rhymes and a writing lesson, lunch, and afternoon assembly, before returning home. For outdoor free play, the children could choose among elaborate playground equipment, including swings, slides, climbing apparatus, merry-go-rounds, tricycles, wagons, and kiddy cars. The stationary playground equipment was clustered together in a small grassy area bordered by trees, shrubs, and beds of flowers. There were several grassy areas surrounded by low hedges and flower beds with gravel walks between them in the style of formal Italian gardens. The children were permitted to play only in the small area where the stationary equipment was located unless they wished to use the wheeled toys, which could be used only on the gravel walk ways.

Experimental Models

The Indian government in conjunction with the states has experimented with different models for delivering services to preschool children. In the states of Tamil Nadu and Madras, a model for low-cost preschool care in rural areas has been developed.[22] Local women with primary education are given a short orientation course and are assisted in running Balwadis in their own villages. While the quality of educational services varies, this model represents an attempt to make preschool education available on a widespread basis to rural families. In the state of Maharashtra, a new kind of preschool institution, *Vikaswadi*, has been developed. The Vikaswadi is a crèche, a Balwadi, and a primary school integrated into one organizational unit.

Since 1969, a network of day care centers called "mobile crèches" has served children of migrant construction workers in Delhi.[23] These crèches, developed under the leadership of Meeva Madevan, recognize the mobility of children who follow their parents from one construction site to another. In 1970, there were five crèches at individual sites in the Delhi area. These centers provide a program of education, health services, and feeding for children from birth to eleven years, at which age most children enter the labor force. The younger children are provided with breakfast and lunch, as well as cleaning and pediatric services. Older children are taught to sing and dance, to paint, and to engage in activities similar to those of nursery school students. Some crèches also function as community centers where films are shown, continuing education for adults is provided, and family-planning activities occur. The mobile crèches are supported under Indian law by the owners of the construction firms, who provide temporary housing or tents, pay salaries, and cover the cost of utilities. Other expenses are paid from public donations. The mobile crèche relies heavily on the voluntary services of foreign and Indian women.

Another innovative program for preschool education in India attached preprimary classes to primary schools. In the state of Rahasthan, the primary first-grade class is reduced to a half-day session, thus releasing the teacher to teach a preschool class. Teachers are given a short orientation with regular in-service training. The purpose of this experiment is to familiarize the preschool children with the teacher, school, and program and to provide continuity in teachers over the two-year period. It is hoped that the experiment will introduce the teacher to new methods and ideas in early education which will be carried over into the primary grades.[24] Another state, Maharashtra, has also begun a program of attaching preprimary classes to primary units for the purposes of teacher training.

Parent and Community Involvement

Unlike early childhood educators in other Asian countries, those in India express great concern about strategies for encouraging parent and community involvement in the preschools, which are seen by some as instruments for social change. The rationale for community participation in preschool education has been presented by Mina Swaminathan.[25] In summary, she emphasizes that (1) the community must be involved during the critical and formative period of the child's life, (2) since the curriculum of the preschool is life itself, the community and its people can contribute resources toward the building of preschools, (3) the bridge between home and school is part of the preschool curriculum, (4) the preschool has the potential to become the basis of social change, and (5) the entire community—not only the parents—must participate toward the optimal development of its children.

Although preschool educators emphasize the importance of parent and community involvement, this participation has been extremely difficult to implement in practice. Preschool education is often seen by parents as an institutional service which removes the child from home for a brief period of group experience. The nature of this group experience differs with the background of the parents. In urban centers serving middle-class children, there is a demand for the provision of an academic curriculum. In rural areas, a preschool which does not appear to serve an academic function becomes a custodial institution. Children attend when care is not available at home, often with little consistency. The difficulties of setting up rural preschools have been analyzed by Khalakdina.[26] Often, differing expectations of the programs by teachers, parents, and community lead to the sacrifice of educational components or of the program itself.

The nature of parent participation differs according to the school and its philosophy. Indira Swaminathan has described some parent participation projects, including group discussions on children and their needs, interests, and problems; courses in child psychology and child observation; participation as an aide; and creating activities and materials for the children.[27] However, these kinds of parent activities are directed mainly toward educated, middle-class mothers, typically in urban areas in demonstration schools. However, Mina Swaminathan has carried out successful projects in cooperative nursery schools in a rural suburb of Delhi which served lower-middle-class families.[28] In the rural areas, community and parent participation on the whole has proved difficult to implement, since the purposes of the preschool are not clearly understood. Many of the mothers have household duties, as well as outside employment, which restrict their full involvement.

RESEARCH AND FUTURE DIRECTIONS

India has an active group of researchers working on educational problems. Studies reflect an interest in providing developmental norms (such as those based on Gesell's work) covering motor, perceptual, cognitive, language, and social development of Indian children from 2½ to 5 years.[29] The work of Rajalakshmi Muralidharan is rich in detailing the development of Indian children from different areas of the country, as well as documenting the family background and conditions of life for the children. Activities are also centered on modifying non-Indian tests for children.[30]

Research on preschool programs has also been conducted. Leela Prem Das conducted a study of preschool facilities, equipment, methods, and curriculum in Delhi.[31] A similar survey was carried out by Anita Verma on the preschools in Baroda.[32] Also, an investigation using a case study approach was conducted on social adjustment of children in a preschool program.[33] Research has also focused on the behavior of children from different socioeconomic backgrounds in the nursery school setting.[34]

There is concern that much of the research literature which is used in courses on child development and in teacher training is based on Western societies having different social, cultural, and economic conditions. Hence, the findings may not be applicable to development of programs for young children in India. Therefore, the Study Group on the Development of the Preschool Child recommended research which would aid in the introduction of truly Indian programs. In its report, the study group recommended the following areas for research activity:[35]

1 A study of the perceptions of teacher educators and supervisors regarding the concept and importance of preschool education, in order to evolve suitable programs for their orientation

2 Parental expectations of preschool education

3 Expectations of primary schools in regard to preschools

4 Studies of preprimary schools and Balwadis situated in different types of socioeconomic areas in order to study:

   a Problems of organization and administration

   b Insights of teachers and aspirations of parents in regard to preschool education

   c Efficiency of the institution in terms of accommodation, staff, instructional techniques, play materials, incidence of wastage, and community support

   d Efficiency of different operational models in specific situations

   e Criteria for the content and presentation of literature for preschool children

   f Type and kind of parent-community participation for various models

5 Studies of preprimary teacher-training institutions and preschool centers which are known to have introduced innovations and succeeded in evolving new patterns of preschool education

6 Action research projects for evolving new models of preschool centers, Balwadis, and training centers for preschool instructors in order to identify administrative, financial, instructional, and other factors involved in their effective organization in accordance with given objectives

7 Child-rearing practices in different regions in the country with special emphasis on sociocultural indices, such as training for independence, competitiveness, family and individual egocentrism, and in relation to later achievement

8 Parent expectations and satisfactions with the preschool development programs, in terms of the socialization process

9 Primary school performance (mental and social indices) of children with and without preschool institutional experiences; developmental

levels of institutional children versus family-reared children in the age group from birth to six years

10 Different systems of preschool education in relation to achievement in later years

In summary, the study group advocated a built-in program of evaluation of all child-care and education activities. Needed research would be carried out by centers already engaged in research, such as the National Center for Educational Research and Training (NCERT), the Indian Council of Social Science Research, state institutes of education, schools of social work, departments of child development in home science colleges, and other preprimary training institutions.

In addition, the Study Group on the Development of the Preschool Child has developed an action program for preschool children through the mobilization of local resources, especially in the rural areas. The report, which was completed in 1972, outlined several areas of needed action:

1 Expansion of programs to cover a significant proportion of vulnerable groups of children. While preschool education was seen as desirable for all children, the need for governmental action was especially great for children in urban slums, children of underprivileged groups in rural areas, and children in isolated tribal areas.

2 Remedying the extreme imbalance in the distribution of child services from state to state, between urban areas and rural and tribal areas, and between privileged and underprivileged groups in urban areas.

3 Better coordination and sharing among the various agencies involved so that the services reach the child in an integrated program. Provision of health, nutrition, recreation, welfare, and education services is often isolated and piecemeal. Hence, an integrated program combining these services with parent and community education was seen as necessary for the total development of the young child.

4 Expansion and reorientation of the training program. The state of teacher training has been described previously. In implementing the plan for community support and involvement in preschool education, the study group recommended the training of paraprofessionals and local women and the part-time employment of educated women and students.

In outlining the models for preschool education, the study group emphasized the importance of local conditions and the need for flexible plans. The group suggested five operational models for demonstration purposes:

1 Full-day, comprehensive day care centers for three- to five-year-olds in urban, low-income areas where both parents work. Integrated services would be provided.

2 Half-day Balwadis for urban and rural areas also offering integrated services.

3 First-stage centers for a few hours a day developed around existing community facilities such as maternal and child health centers.

4 Anganwadis for rural areas offering two to four hours of nutrition, recreation, and education daily.

5 Primary-school-based centers for children who will enter primary grades within a year, with recreation and school readiness activities. These classes would be taught by a primary teacher who would obtain released time from her teaching duties.

At present, the combined efforts of public and private agencies reach approximately 2 percent of the three- to five-year-olds in the country. The study group projected an expansion to 5 million children by 1981. However, given the critical importance of health and nutritional services to Indian children, it does not appear likely that educational components will be expanded for many children. Future directions in preschool education appear to include means of finding low-cost approaches to bring health, nutrition, schooling, and adult and parent education into the preschool thrust. The coordination of the numerous agencies now involved in the care and education of children remains a significant problem.

In summary, the major obstacle to Indian preschool expansion is limited resources—financial, human, and material. However, the commitment of the early education professional field to the expansion and improvement of programs is strong. Many national organizations such as the Indian Association for Preschool Education (IAPE), the Indian Federation of Pre-Primary Institutions, the Children's Education Societies and Trusts, and the Child Study in the National Center for Educational Research and Training (NCERT) will, as in the past, continue to give needed impetus to expand services for Indian children.

NOTES

1 R. H. Dave, "Directions and Dynamics of Educational Change in India," *UCLA Educator*, vol. 17, pp. 25–30, Fall 1974.

2 National Center for Educational Research and Training, *Indian Yearbook of Education, Second Yearbook: Elementary Education*, New Delhi, 1964, p. 21.

3   Dave, op. cit., p. 27.

4   Ibid., p. 30.

5   UNESCO, *Statistical Yearbook, 1971,* UNESCO, Paris, 1972, p. 111.

6   For a discussion of Montessori's influence in India, see Sol Cohen, "Maria Montessori: Priestess or Pedagogue?" *Teachers College Record,* vol. 71, pp. 314-326, December 1969.

7   A detailed description of prebasic education can be found in G. Pankajan, "Classroom Practices in Pre-Basic School," *NIE Journal,* vol. 5, pp. 52-56, 1970.

8   Ministry of Education (India), *First Yearbook: A Review of Education in India, 1947-61,* Government of India, New Delhi, 1961.

9   Margaret Khalakdina, "The Preschool in Rural India," *NIE Journal,* vol. 5, p. 45, 1970.

10 Mina Swaminathan, "The Preschool Child in India," *Assignment Children,* vol. 21, p. 3, Jan.-March 1973.

11 Ibid. See also, S. Panandikar, "The Place of Preschool Education in the Educational System," *NIE Journal,* vol. 5, pp. 7-9, 1970 and Anita Verma, "The Role of a Laboratory Nursery School," *NIE Journal,* vol. 5, pp. 24-29, 1970.

12 Indira Swaminathan, "Preschool Education, Parents, and Community in a Developing Society," *NIE Journal,* vol. 5, pp. 33-39, 1970; Mina Swaminathan, "Community Participation in Preschool Education—Why and How," *NIE Journal,* vol. 5, pp. 18-23, 1970.

13 Khalakdina, op. cit., p. 48.

14 S. Kumar, "Pre-primary Education in India since 1947—An Appraisal," *Indian Education,* vol. 7, p. 6, April 1968.

15 Ministry of Education and Social Welfare (India), *Report of the Study Group on the Development of the Preschool Child,* New Dehli, 1972, pp. 8-12.

16 Mina Swaminathan, "The Preschool Child in India," op. cit., p. 11.

17 Ministry of Education and Social Welfare (India), op. cit., pp. 26-33.

18 Mina Swaminathan, "The Preschool Child in India," op. cit., p. 11.

19 Central Social Welfare Board (India), *Organization of a Rural Balwadi,* Government of India, New Delhi, 1965, pp. 2-3.

20 Margaret Varma, "Human Relations Laboratory," *NIE Journal,* vol. 5, p. 30, 1970.

21 Servants are not assistant teachers. Assistant teachers in India have the same role and functions as head teachers only with less overall responsibility for planning, organizing curriculum, supervision, and teaching. Servants never teach. They clean up, assist with lunch or snack and with toileting, or supervise recess. They do not lead any activities, even

outdoor games. Servants, children, and teachers all know and respect
their roles and each other, and all tend to treat each other with mutual
warmth and affection.

22 Mina Swaminathan, "The Preschool Child in India," op. cit.

23 Meeva Madevan, "Preschool Education for the Poor—A Personal Testi-
mony," *Report of the Seminar on the Pre-School Child,* Madras, India,
December 14-19, 1970, pp. 250-253.

24 Thailand experimented with a similar scheme in the early 1950s.
However, parental pressure and the development needs of the country
tended to favor formal, academic instruction, even at the preschool
level.

25 Mina Swaminathan, "Community Participation in Preschool Education," pp. 18-19.

26 Khalakdina, op. cit.

27 Indira Swaminathan, op. cit., pp. 36-38.

28 Mina Swaminathan, "Community Participation in Preschool Education," op. cit., p. 21.

29 Rajalakshmi Muralidharan, "Developmental Norms of Children Aged
$2\frac{1}{2}$ -5 years: A Pilot Study," *Indian Educational Review,* vol. 4, pp. 67-91,
January 1969; A. Anandalakshmy, "A Perspective on Cognitive Develop-
ment: The Preschool Child's Performance in Classification Tasks," *NIE
Journal,* vol. 5, pp. 57-60, 1970; H. D. Badami, "The Study of Growth
Patterns among the Children under Five Years of Age in Cambay,"
Education and Psychology Review, vol. 4, October 1969.

30 M. Gosh, "Application of Good Enough Test to U.P. Children of Ages
3+ to 10+," *Calcutta Review,* vol. 177, pp. 192-200, December 1965.

31 Leela Prem Das, *Preschool Education in Delhi,* a report of a survey
conducted in 1962, Navin Press, Delhi, 1974, pp. 30-31.

32 Anita Verma, *A Survey of 45 Preschool Institutions in the City of Baroda,*
Department of Child Development, Faculty of Home Science, University of Baroda, India, 1967.

33 E. A. Pires and Usha Kanwar, *First Steps in the Socialization of Children
in the CIE Nursery School,* Central Institute of Education (India), Delhi,
1958.

34 H. K. Nijahawan, "Relationship of Children's Ages, Parents' Income and
Occupations to Observed Patterns of Nursery School Behavior," *Indian
Journal of Applied Psychology,* vol. 5, pp. 23-31, January 1968; K. Patel,
"A Comparison of English Speaking and Non-English Speaking Nursery
School Children in English Medium Schools in India," *Journal of
Psychological Researches,* vol. 9, pp. 102-108, September 1965.

35 Ministry of Education and Social Welfare (India), op. cit., pp. 37-38.

CHAPTER 9

FUTURE DIRECTIONS

Distinguished historians such as Bernard Bailyn and Lawrence Cremin have extended the setting associated with education from the school to nonschool agencies such as families, religious organizations, working places, and other sites of community and group activity.[1] They broaden the definition of education to include processes of cultural transmission or as Cremin defines it, "the deliberate, systematic, and sustained effort to transmit, evoke, or acquire knowledge, values, attitudes, skills and sensibilities."[2] Early schooling must also be considered in this context. Another significant aspect of Cremin's developing theory of education for the study of early schooling is his notion of "configurations of education."[3] That is, educational institutions at any given time and place relate to each other in changing configurations which are associated with the changing allocation of educational functions among them. In periods of social change, these configurations shift and, as a result, raise questions regarding the educational functions of any one institution. In any given society, for example, proposed expansion of preschools and child-care facilities may not be hotly debated, depending on whether the balance between familial and outside agencies is changing in regard to the allocation of responsibility for educational functions. Thus, early schooling as an area of inquiry must be expanded beyond the professionals who relate directly to children to include those who focus on the social, economic, political, and cultural networks which affect the nature of life for families in any society. Therefore, this discussion of future directions for inquiry is directed toward a broad constituency—early education specialists, social welfare advocates, health-related professionals, legislators, parents, and psychologists, as well as scholars in the areas listed above.

NOTE: This chapter extends ideas originally presented in Ruby Takanishi, "Early Child Care and Education in Cross-National Perspective," *Review of Education*, vol. 1, no. 4, 1975.

The findings of cross-national research can be seen as serving two purposes. First, they can provide models for practice within a country. Second, cross-national research can illuminate our understanding of national traditions, social mores, and indigenous practices by placing them in a comparative context. Such research might provide explanatory principles for understanding patterns of education, worldwide. Most of the discussion in this chapter is devoted to the second purpose. However, a brief discussion—and caution—relating to the first is in order.

The practice of looking to other countries for models and guidance regarding the care and education of children within one's own country has a rich historical tradition. At the turn of the century, visitors crossed the Atlantic in both directions to exchange ideas regarding the problems of juvenile delinquency, child labor, and early education. American social reformers concerned about vagrant youth traveled to England, Germany, and Switzerland. The settlement houses of kindergartens at the turn of the century were modeled after English and Swiss attempts. The American programs and practices which emerged, however, took on a character shaped by local conditions. The question not often addressed by the Asian countries, except perhaps by India, is how one develops programs, curricula, and practices which are linked to native culture and local conditions of life.

For example, the relatively recent development of multicultural and bilingual programs for American children from minority groups may provide an impetus for Asian countries with heterogeneous populations to experiment with early schooling programs which meet the needs of children from diverse backgrounds. However, the development of these programs will depend on a country's priorities for the development of national unity. The relevant lesson may come from the American experience at the turn of the century, when the need to assimilate large numbers of immigrants led to an emphasis on programs aimed at developing a national culture rather than the culturally pluralistic society which is currently advocated by some educators. In the Asian countries, the potential for utilizing early schooling to promote national unity is only just emerging and should be watched closely, especially in Malaysia and India, both of which are composed of varied ethnic and cultural groups. In Thailand, preschool education is being implemented in the northern provinces on a very limited scale as one governmental strategy for integrating isolated tribal groups into the Thai nation.

We must also be prepared to expect different kinds of relationships among countries. For example, there appear to be some intriguing differences in the relationship between the entry of women into the labor force and the expansion of preschools. While in the United States and in many of the Eastern European countries after the Second World War the availability of child care and education outside the home has been related to increases in the numbers of working women, in the Netherlands this relationship does not hold. While the proportion of women in the Dutch labor force is still relatively small, preschools are available for almost every child who wishes to enroll. Also, as Papanek suggests, "Negative relationships often found between female labor force participation and the number of children a woman has may not hold for Asian societies." Reasons include the availability of cheap domestic help, extended family residential patterns, more flexible hours of employment, and compatibility between child care and work patterns.[4] Thus a major expansion in preschool facilities in Asia may occur for very different reasons than it has in many countries of the West.

In addition, a number of societal and cultural factors in which the working woman is embedded condition this relationship. With changing social and economic conditions, women's views of their roles may change in directions which are not predicted by the feminist movements. In postwar Japan, for example, women were expected both to work and to administer a household and family. However, with increasing economic prosperity and recovery, there has been a movement back to the home and children among some segments of the population.

FUTURE DIRECTIONS FOR INQUIRY

Large-scale cross-national inquiries into early schooling have been under way for almost a decade. An overview of this activity was provided in Chapter 1. This volume on seven Asian countries expands the coverage which heretofore has been available on the United States, various European countries (including the U.S.S.R.), Israel, and the People's Republic of China. Little information is currently available on the countries of Africa and South America, where early schooling is still in the beginning stages of development.

It seems worthwhile now to outline some future directions for inquiry based on our own work and that of others. In the following discussion, we suggest needed improvements in existing demographic and descriptive cross-national research on early schooling and also the need to go beyond these demographic and descriptive studies in order to examine systematically the factors which are related to the status, structure, content, and methods of early schooling in a given country.

The Demography of Early Schooling

In presenting statistical information on early schooling in each Asian country, we noted the difficulties in obtaining accurate figures on facilities, enrollment, and teachers according to program sponsorship. The last international survey of preprimary education was conducted in 1960 by the International Bureau of Education and UNESCO.[5] Since that time, there have been a number of conferences on preschool education, but little current information on the demography of early schooling on an international basis has been available.

In view of the increasing significance of early schooling in national policy discussions, it is necessary that another international survey of early schooling be conducted to provide information on the status of programs in individual countries. Such information needs to be updated continually. Agencies such as UNESCO which now conduct educational surveys on an annual basis should make renewed efforts both in defining early schooling and in collecting data to provide more detailed information on preprimary education, including programs for infants and toddlers. The distinction between child-care or day care facilities with a custodial or health focus and preschools with an educational focus should be reconsidered in the context of a broader definition of education, as suggested by Lawrence Cremin. In any case, statistical information on child-care units should be included in the annual surveys, not excluded as is the current practice. Basic demographic information which should be collected includes the number of facilities, children, and teachers by program sponsorship; governmental regulations of different aspects of facilities; the ages of the children served, beginning at birth, and the number of children served at each age; characteristics of the children who are enrolled, including their ethnic background, socioeconomic status, residence (urban or rural), and how their eligibility for programs is defined (low income, industry related, handicapped, minority group); the nature of the services provided; a description of teacher training and certification; and staffing patterns, including the teacher-child ratio and auxiliary staff members.

Demographic information provides only descriptive data on the status of early schooling. Such information tells us little about the factors and processes which led to the development of these characteristics of early schooling in a given country. However, without good demographic data, our attempts to examine these factors do not rest on firm ground. Thus, demography of early schooling serves as a starting point for our attempts to understand the complexity of conditions which are related to the development and provision of early schooling programs.

The Need for Descriptive Frameworks

As we pointed out in Chapter 1, a large number of descriptive cross-national studies of early schooling have been conducted. However, in most of the work on early schooling, the framework which organizes the inquiry is left implicit. Typically, the professional and disciplinary training of the worker influences what is seen and what is chosen for presentation. Hence, a critical problem in cross-national inquiry lies in the formulation of frameworks which will systematize the description of the social context as well as of children's programs. A number of recent books in the field provide examples of descriptive frameworks for the cross-national study of early care and education. The International Monograph Series on Early Child Care,[6] edited by Halbert B. Robinson and Nancy M. Robinson, first appeared as special issues of the *Early Child Development and Care* journal and was then published in book form. In early 1975, monographs were available on Hungary, Sweden, the United States, Switzerland, Britain, and France. Each monograph is written according to a common outline and provides information on the history and the political, economic, and social structure of the country; prevailing conceptions of the child and the child-rearing process; the nature of the compact between the family and the society in early socialization; social planning for children and families; descriptions of specific socialization settings and processes, including the family, schools, and programs; training of personnel who work with children; children's television, books, toys, and other media; dissemination of information about child development and rearing; research on child development and preschool programs; and finally, future directions for programs. This outline is a comprehensive one and a good beginning for individuals undertaking descriptive studies of early schooling. It provides, at least, a common basis of information for future discussion.

In their study of American early schooling, Goodlad and his associates went "behind nursery school doors" and found an "incongruity between nursery schools as they exist and ideas and practices considered to be at the forefront of research and theory."[7] Program description is not an easy task even in one's own country. Problems reflect the nature of the preschool field and include: (1) differences in conceptualizations of the child and related theories of development, (2) different societal goals regarding the function of preschool education, and (3) slippage between espoused goals and actual implementation, resulting in variations in programs actually experienced by children. These problem areas must be taken seriously in descriptions of programs within countries. Susan Jacoby's description of urban Soviet schools is a telling example and warning for those who would make generalizations based on visiting a small sample of schools even in a highly centralized educational system.[8] She noted differences in administration, leadership, goals, teacher morale and behavior, classroom climate, and student activity among the Moscow schools. Her description is significant in the sense that we have often referred to the "Soviet schools" as if they represented a single entity.

Difficulties in program description are partly related to the underdeveloped state of the art in American research. There is a great deal of research on American early education programs which focuses on child outcomes. On the other hand, relatively few research studies have been conducted which attempt to link program goals; their implementation in the physical and social environment of the classroom; classroom processes, including teacher-child, child-child, and child-environment interactions; and related child outcomes. Program variation is a reality of the early education field, as it is of other levels, yet we know little regarding the measurement and meaning of this variation.

Cross-national researchers face the task of developing methods which can aid in the systematic observation of programs for children. Observational procedures for programs are a relatively recent development, and it will be worthwhile to consider whether procedures based on American programs are directly applicable in other countries, given the potentially different goals and meanings of behavior which an observer may encounter.

We encountered several examples in our own work. One of the most salient observations was the almost universal tendency to group children for activities. American early education places a great deal of emphasis on social development, especially in learning to work and play in group settings. Since American children are most often raised in the environment of the nuclear family, the nursery school often provides the first context for the development of social skills and preparation for future experience in group settings. However, American educators also place a great deal of importance on the development of individuality and, successfully or unsuccessfully, attempt to provide activities to promote it.

On the other hand, in Japanese society, social development is related to preparation for the constant presence and pressures of group life which are found in the social and economic spheres in adulthood. Thus, while an American observer may note that the Japanese nursery schools do not promote individuality, as evidenced by lack of emphasis on independent activities and time for "being alone," these very activities may be seen as inconsistent with expectations for competent adult behavior. Clearly, the goals and values for early schooling need to be examined within the specific societal and cultural context before conducting observational studies of early schooling programs.

Cross-national descriptive studies are difficult to conduct and interpret, since in many countries regional variations and related beliefs and practices make it difficult to discern a national pattern, if such an entity exists. The issue of diversity *within* a given country has rarely been addressed, since the global concepts of "culture" and "national character" have been used as if they referred to homogeneous entities. However, there have been recent developments which indicate that intranational variation will receive greater attention in the future. In the sixth volume of the International Monograph Series on early child care in France, Myriam David and Irene Lezine state that "France is a nation of extreme diversities. This is true in geography and terrain, in its economic organization, and its diverse subcultural groups. Not only are there strong contrasts between one region and another, one group and another—but there are also contrasts and inconsistencies within groups. The political and ideological orientation of different groups conflict, and so do their views on children, families, and the process of education."[9]

Intranational controversy and conflict regarding the care and education of children outside the family has not been carefully examined in many countries, including the United States. Undertaking such an examination presents conceptual as well as methodological problems. Since most human beings have been raised in families, it is a difficult area in which to conduct a nonemotional investigation. Furthermore, expressed values and behavior are often unrelated. Use of classification categories such as ethnicity and social class often assumes a homogeneity of values which does not exist.

Within the Asian context, one might make two rough levels of distinction in group differences regarding the child and the family. First, countries vary in the number of ethnic groups which make up the population and the extent to which these groups have maintained their separateness. Thus countries can be distinguished by relative ethnic heterogeneity (e.g., India, Malaysia, the Philippines, and Thailand)[10] or homogeneity (Japan, Hong Kong, and Korea). Second, even within countries which appear to be composed of one ethnic group, there are often important regional and ideological differences which must be taken into account in the study of within-country variation in the views of family and children. What this suggests is that we must see the problems of child care and education not solely from the level of children and families but also in the context within which each country structures and changes its social, economic, and political relations. We must begin to examine the dynamics and politics of early schooling program planning, implementation, and coordination.[11] If it is true that policy-level problems regarding early schooling are shared in many countries, the way in which each country attempts to solve these problems is a critical area for inquiry.

The provision of services and programs for children and families is a political problem which integrally involves social values, philosophy, economic constraints, and to some extent research evidence. Program development is a dynamic process in which overt and hidden conflicts over societal goals and the role of the family come to a head. In most Asian countries, except for Japan, a national priority has been placed on the achievement of universal primary education. As a result, preschools have been slow to develop except in the private sector and in special government-supported programs which serve national needs.

Tradition is another factor which determines provision of programs. In Japan, for example, formal education is traditionally assumed to begin at age six, even though cross-national surveys have indicated that the age of beginning schooling may vary anywhere from five to eight. Clearly, historical precedents and the society's view of the child enter into decisions regarding the age of beginning formal schooling, whether or not research evidence is available.

The role of the family in early socialization of the child is often a critical issue, at least in Western countries. In the United States, political opposition to the expansion of early schooling programs has centered on the resistance to communal child-rearing schemes. In other countries, especially those with strong religious orientations, the family, or more precisely the mother, is seen to be the most important influence in the young child's life. This issue may not be so critical in some Asian countries where definitions of the family extend beyond the nuclear unit and where children are sometimes expected to live with relatives and other members of the defined family network. Christopher Lasch warns that it is hazardous to generalize from Western societies to Asian countries regarding conditions leading to changes in the functions and meaning of various family structures.[12]

Perhaps the most important question revolves around the role of the state in programs relating to the upbringing of young children. Even in countries where the prevailing political ideology supports a concept of the state as a primary socializing agent, as in the socialist countries, there is often a delicate balance between the functions of the family and those of the state. Sweden provides an example of the concept of "family support systems" which do not directly intervene in family life but provide for the health, housing, and economic security of children and families. The question of what role the state should play in upbringing vis-à-vis other agencies such as the church and the family remains an important area for inquiry.

What is needed then are public policy analyses of child-care and education programs in individual countries. Except perhaps for the International Monograph Series volume on Sweden, there has been little work in this area. In addition, a historical perspective on the development of programs in a country could provide an understanding of the factors which contribute to the development of early schooling as an educational agency.

TOWARD INTERPRETIVE STUDIES

The influence of the social context on the processes of early socialization is not unidirectional. The influence of the social and physical environment is mediated by individuals and may have different outcomes depending on how those individuals perceive their environment and values. To place this argument in a theoretical perspective, Clifford Geertz has made a case for an "interpretive theory of culture."[13] He argues that the major focus of a semiotic approach to culture is to gain access to the "conceptual world" of individuals, that is, to understand the world as individuals construct and define it in the "informal logic of life."[14]

This interpretive approach has several implications for inquiry in cross-national studies. The first major implication is that researchers must not assume that similar events or objects have similar meaning for individuals both in different cultures and in the same culture. For example, as indicated earlier, what may appear to Americans to be highly regimented daily activities in some Asian preschool settings may be as important a socialization goal of Asian teachers as the development of individuality is to American teachers. In Hong Kong and the Republic of China, children performed highly intricate dances and plays often accompanied by group singing. Some American observers may label these activities as "structured," meaning that they are initiated and directed by the teacher and follow prescribed, often step-by-step renditions of movements and language which are part of the cultural tradition. These structured activities are often seen as antithetical to free play, creativity, and independence, which are highly valued by many American early educators. However, in the context of Chinese culture, the mastery of these traditional arts among the young is integrally tied to societal definitions of desired competency.

A further caution is that definitions of similar words such as "independence," "self-reliance," and "free play" may be imbued with different meanings in each country. Hence, in future cross-national studies of early schooling, an exploration of the meaning and practice of preschool goals needs to be undertaken. Translation of words may be only the first step in this understanding. Many times in examining and presenting the goals of early schooling in chapters in this book, we have puzzled over their meaning as translated into the values and behaviors of the teachers.

Socialization goals become operational through the teachers' interpretation of the nature of the society and the roles which children in the society must master to become adult members. One hypothesis which could be explored is the extent to which early schooling constitutes a "miniature society" modeled after contexts, attitudes, and behaviors which are indicative of adult competence in a country. Another hypothesis which could be fruitfully examined is how the segregation of preschool children by social class in many countries may give rise to different anticipatory socialization practices for children from many different social strata.[15]

In examining the conceptualizations of the child in a given country, the survey and questionnaire method may be of limited value in finding out what people think about children and how they translate their beliefs into their ongoing interaction with children. It may well be that how researchers and native child specialists conceptualize children is different from that of parents and other care givers who rely on "folk wisdom" transmitted in the culture from one generation to the next through noninstitutional networks. In Hungary, for example, professionals have attempted to change child-rearing practices, most notably the use of physical punishment. However, surveys based on parental reports indicate that this practice is still used by a significant minority of Hungarian families. Likewise, research findings regarding rapid change and learning during the first year of life have not appeared to affect the Hungarian pediatrics field.[16] While research has implicitly focused on what parents should believe about child rearing and the nature of development, we know relatively little about what parents actually believe—parental wisdom—and somewhat less about what they actually do on a day-to-day basis. What this suggests is that conceptual developments in the field of socialization and child rearing need to be closely integrated into cross-national studies of early schooling.[17] Socialization can be reconceptualized as a reciprocal "process of mutual influence bound to the relative 'objectivity' of the society, a process through which the generations construct and reconstruct social reality,"[18] and in which children can influence the values, attitudes, and skills of adults, including their own parents.

Another promising area for inquiry related to an interpretive approach is the possible existence of a culture of teachers of young children. Lilian G. Katz begins to address this issue when she argues for a reorientation of research and development in early childhood education:

> The basic aim has been to translate theory into practice, a traditional approach to curriculum development. The reorientation I would like to propose is that of conducting more research on practice. That is to say, rather than asking how research on child development can be translated into curriculum models we might ask: What are the factors which either inhibit or facilitate the implementation of our ideas, knowledge, and curriculum models?[19]

In advocating a "sociology of early education," Katz points to the importance of social contexts in which teachers of young children work. This is an untapped area within the early schooling field, though a substantial body of research with a similar focus exists for elementary and secondary schooling.[20] This work provides an important reference point for beginning inquiry. However, there are possibly important differences between the early schooling field and elementary and secondary education, e.g., in professional norms, credential requirements, and educational philosophy. The current focus on providing continuity or articulating preschool and primary units indicates that such differences are significant.

Part of the theory-into-practice gap which the leading educators bemoan on an international basis may be related to our limited understanding of what teachers of preschool children believe about children and their development, and their understanding of why they engage in certain practices. Along these lines, Philip Jackson's study *Life in Classrooms* represents a model of inquiry for examining life in early schooling units.[21]

Not only do we need to learn more about how programs provide similar and dissimilar experiences for children in different countries, we also need to understand the influence of the experiences on children. This is an undeveloped state of knowledge both in the United States and throughout the world. Assumptions about the social and educational functions of preschools indicate that, depending on the country, early schooling experience develops dedicated socialist citizens, will alleviate economic and social inequities in succeeding generations, and is critical for the future development of young children. However, there is a paucity of evidence to support these claims. In addition, early schooling must be considered as only one of the many education agencies which influence children in any society. Thus, we may have to change our justifications for preschool education.

TOWARD NEW METHODOLOGIES

In addressing the issue of "realizable aspirations for social science inquiry," Lee J. Cronbach argues that "the special task of the social scientist is to pin down contemporary facts,"[22] that is, to study carefully each particular program, taking into account factors unique to that situation. He adds, "As [the researcher] goes from situation to situation, his first task is to describe and interpret the effect anew in each locale, perhaps taking into account factors unique to that locale or series of events."[23]

Instead of aiming to make our findings suitable for generalization, we must use them as hypotheses to be tested in new situations. When local conditions are assessed in depth, we may be in a better position to understand the factors which led to the situation and those which will facilitate or obstruct its development.

Clearly, research methods based on the natural sciences must be modified and, in some cases, new methods developed. However, we suspect that to discuss methodology before conceptual analysis is somewhat premature. A beginning analysis would address itself to questions such as: What is the suitability of the program to local community and, in some cases, cultural conditions? What are the relationships of the program to other educational agencies (both public and private) in the community? What is the community's perception of the program? What are the variations in the community and on what factors is this variation based? How may such factors as the availability of physical space and materials affect program delivery? Finally, who are the individuals involved, especially those who direct the program? What are their leadership styles, their abilities to provide linkages with other agencies, and their skills in developing and maintaining staff morale? What these questions suggest is that in-depth examinations of small numbers of programs in each country will provide a better understanding of early schooling as it actually operates than studies which attempt to provide a "global" overall picture which may not characterize any single program in the country.

A case study approach to early schooling using ethnographic methods developed in anthropology is one methodology which could be used.[24] Early schooling in any country is not a monolithic entity, and attempts to describe it as such lead to a descriptive collage which is not necessarily representative of any given program. Ethnographic methods also hold the promise that the social context of early schooling will be more systematically explored than in the past.

In addition to anthropological contributions, some "sociological imagination"[25] will also be essential. That is, we need to link what happens within families and in preschools to the social conditions which surround them. Psychologists can play an important role by attempting to understand how individuals mediate the influence of social conditions. It is clear that cross-national research on early schooling must engage the interest of diverse disciplines in order to develop in the future.

In this final chapter, we have focused our attention on directions for cross-national research on early schooling. While we are well aware that research, although it does play a part, is not a significant determinant of how a society chooses to socialize its children, we do believe that well-conceptualized research can help us clarify and understand the nature of early schooling in a given country as it is viewed in the eyes of the society and its agents and as it is experienced by children. It is this kind of understanding which holds the promise that what is learned from cross-national exchange will enhance the developmental potential of children in their own communities throughout the world.

NOTES

1   Bernard Bailyn, *Education in the Forming of American Society,* Vintage, New York, 1960; and Lawrence A. Cremin, "Further Notes toward a Theory of Education," *Notes on Education,* no. 4, p. 1, Institute of Philosophy and Politics of Education, Teachers College, Columbia University, New York, March 1974.

2   Lawrence A. Cremin, "Notes toward a Theory of Education," *Notes on Education,,* no. 1, pp. 4-5, Institute of Philosophy and Politics of Education, Teachers College, Columbia University, New York, June 1973.

3   Cremin, ibid.

4   Hanna Papanek, "Women in South and Southeast Asia: Issues and Research," *Signs* (Journal of Women in Culture and Society), vol. 1, no. 1, p. 198, Autumn 1975.

5   International Bureau of Education and UNESCO, *Organization of Preprimary Education,* XXIVth International Congress on Public Education, Geneva, 1961.

6   Halbert B. Robinson and Nancy M. Robinson, eds., *International Monograph Series on Early Child Care,* Gordon and Breach, New York, 1972. (Continuing.)

7   John I. Goodlad, M. Frances Klein, Jerrold M. Novotney, and Associates, *Early Schooling in the United States,* McGraw-Hill, New York, 1973, p. 123.

8   Susan Jacoby, *Inside Soviet Schools,* Hill and Wang, New York, 1974.

9   Myriam David and Irene Lezine, *Early Child Care in France,* Gordon and Breach, New York, 1975, p. 2.

10   Although Thailand was referred to in Chapter 7 as relatively culturally homogeneous, it should be noted that it is made up of many diverse ethnic groups.

11   For an example of an examination of the politics of federal involvement in American early education see, Ruby Takanishi, "Federal Involvement in Early Childhood Education (1933-1973): The Need for Historical Perspectives," in Lilian G. Katz (ed.), *Current Topics in Early Childhood Education,* vol. 1, 1976.

12 Christopher Lasch, "The Family and History," *New York Review of Books,* vol. XXII, no. 18, p. 38, November 13, 1975.

13 Clifford Geertz, *The Interpretation of Cultures,* Basic Books, New York, 1973, chapter 1.

14 Ibid., p. 17.

15 This thesis was advanced in Ruth Bettelheim, "Futures of the Unborn: Political, Economic, and Educational Socialization in Asian Preschools," unpublished doctoral dissertation, University of California, Los Angeles, 1972.

16 Alice Hermann and Sandor Komlosi, *Early Child Care in Hungary,* Gordon and Breach, New York, 1973.

17 Kurt K. Lüscher, Verena Ritter, and Peter Gross, *Early Child Care in Switzerland,* Gordon and Breach, New York, 1973. See also Hope Jensen Leichter, "Some Perspectives on the Family as Educator," *Teachers College Record,* vol. 76, pp. 175–217, December 1974.

18 Lüscher, Ritter, and Gross, op. cit., p. 104.

19 Lilian G. Katz, "Where Is Early Childhood Education Going?" *Theory into Practice,* vol. 12, p. 139, 1973.

20 See, for example, Seymour B. Sarason, *The Culture of the School and the Problem of Change,* Allyn and Bacon, Boston, 1971; and Mary M. Bentzen and Associates, *Changing Schools: The Magic Feather Principle,* McGraw-Hill, New York, 1974.

21 Philip Jackson, *Life in Classrooms,* Holt, New York, 1968.

22 Lee J. Cronbach, "Beyond the Two Disciplines of Scientific Psychology," *American Psychologist,* vol. 30, p. 126, February 1975.

23 Ibid., p. 125.

24 Murray L. Wax, Stanley Diamond, and Fred O. Gearing (eds.), *Anthropological Perspectives on Education,* Basic Books, New York, 1971.

25 C. Wright Mills, *The Sociological Imagination,* Oxford University Press, New York, 1959.

APPENDIX A

United Nations Educational, Scientific and Cultural Organization and International Bureau of Education
International Conference on Public Education
Geneva, 1961
Recommendation No. 53 to the Ministries of Education Concerning
the Organization of Pre-primary Education

The International Conference on Public Education,

Convened in Geneva by the United Nations Educational, Scientific and Cultural Organization and the International Bureau of Education, having assembled on the third of July, nineteen hundred and sixty-one, for its twenty-fourth session, adopts on the fourteenth of July, nineteen hundred and sixty-one, the following recommendation:

The Conference,

Considering the principles set forth in Recommendation no. 17 on the organization of pre-primary education, adopted on the nineteenth of July, nineteen hundred and thirty-nine, by the International Conference on Public Education at its eighth session,

Considering the need to provide a child from the earliest age with an education favourable to his full spiritual, moral, intellectual and physical development,

Considering that a young child's early education is both a primary duty and an inalienable right of his parents,

Considering that, although the family remains the most suitable environment for the child's development, parents require assistance, since even under the best of conditions they can no longer meet on their own all the educational needs of the young child when he approaches the age of four,

Considering that, owing to the increase in the number of women who have professional interests and of those who, for various reasons, are overburdened with work at home, pre-primary education increasingly fulfils in modern life a social role in offering the child the security he needs and in taking care of his full development,

Considering that attendance at a pre-primary education establishment facilitates the transition from home to school,

Considering that attendance at a pre-primary education establishment favours the rapid identification of all physical or mental disorders, which can be cured or improved all the more easily if they have been detected as soon as possible, and that it is also very beneficial to physically handicapped children in that it accustoms them at an early age to living with other children,

Considering that the experience so far obtained offers an adequate basis for the formulation of principles and methods of pre-primary education,

Considering that pre-primary education requires of the educators who devote themselves to it both special training and also particular qualities and abilities,

Considering that, in each country, the problem of the extension of pre-primary education seems to be connected with the stage reached in the provision of education for children of school age, and that it is well to take into account the differences which may exist between areas, industrial or rural, where women workers are widely employed and other areas,

Considering that, despite similar aspirations, countries in very different positions must reach varied solutions of the problems of the organization of pre-primary education,

Submits to the Ministries of Education of the different countries the following recommendation:

Possibilities of introducing and extending pre-primary education

1. It is important that the authorities responsible for education should encourage the introduction, extension and progress of pre-primary education, taking into account the stage reached by education in each country and the situation in different localities.

2. Wherever compulsory schooling is already provided for all children without exception, educational facilities should be offered to children of pre-primary age in so far as their numbers justify the opening of an institution or class of the corresponding type.

3. In countries where the provision of compulsory schooling for all has not yet been achieved, it is desirable, while reserving priority for the requirements of the primary school, to take steps for the development of pre-primary education facilities, particularly in industrial areas and in rural areas where women workers are widely employed.

4. It is desirable to take into account the fact that pre-primary education, while retaining its essentially educational character, also meets social needs which are assuming increasing importance in a changing world; for this reason, it is indispensable to achieve very close collaboration between public and private education authorities, the medical and social services and the parents.

5. It is desirable for business concerns and institutions employing women to create and develop pre-primary education establishments in collaboration with the appropriate education authorities.

Administration, supervision and financing

6. In countries where pre-primary education exists, there should be a special department, under the education authorities, to deal with all questions concerning the development and improvement of pre-primary education establishments.

7. The various activities of the special pre-primary education department should include in particular:

(a) a survey of the number of pre-primary age children and of their distribution in relation to the size of the population in their place of residence and to their home environment;

(b) the collection of data on the number and type of pre-primary education establishments in existence, the proportion of public and private establishments in the total, and their attendance rate;

(c) a consideration of the possibilities of extending pre-primary education and plans for this expansion;

(d the study of methodological problems raised by pre-primary education;

(e) an examination of problems related to the selection, training, in-service education and professional status of teaching staff;

(f) the preparation of educational and technical standards and of regulations for the buildings and equipment used for pre-primary education;

(g) the strengthening of collaboration between parents and teachers at pre-primary level.

8. It is the duty of the education authorities to arrange for the educational and health inspection of all pre-primary education establishments, whether public or private.

9. When justified by the numerical importance of pre-primary establishments, their supervision should be carried out by specialized inspectors; in other cases, supervision may be the responsibility of primary school inspectors specially prepared for this work.

10. The method of financing public pre-primary education establishments may vary according to the administrative structure of each country; it is, however, to be hoped that the cost of this type of education will be assumed not only by the local authorities but also by administrative authorities of a higher level.

11. In so far as establishments run by private initiative make up for a shortage of public provision for pre-primary education and offer adequate facilities for education and social welfare, these establishments should be able to count on financial assistance from the authorities.

Structure and organization

12. Notwithstanding the benefit children can derive from attending a pre-primary education establishment, attendance should remain optional.

13. When an establishment is financed entirely by the public authorities, it is desirable that the children should be admitted free of charge.

14. The minimum age for admission to pre-primary education establishments varies with the characteristics of the different types of institution; the leaving age, however, should coincide with the statutory age for entering the primary school.

15. When pre-primary establishments are not numerous enough to accommodate all requests for admission, selection should be based primarily on consideration of the child's individual needs and family circumstances.

16. The number of children per teacher at pre-primary level should be lower than the number of pupils in a primary school class and should be proportionately smaller as the children are younger; it is desirable that the average number of children present should not exceed twenty-five.

17. The teacher should have the aid of an assistant and of essential ancillary staff, especially in establishments where social services are extensively provided.

18. The hours of opening and programme of activities in a pre-primary education establishment should be more flexible than in the primary school, so that they may be adapted as well as possible to the needs of the children and of their families; there may be establishments which are open only in the morning and others which are open all day and provide for the usual meals and indispensable rest periods.

19. In the country and wherever circumstances permit, seasonal pre-primary establishments, which are open while the parents are busy with important agricultural or other work, should become permanent in order to provide for the children's needs all the year round.

Educational activities and techniques

20. Pre-primary education should use methods which take into account the most recent developments in the psychology of the small child and the progress of educational science; these methods will be based on action, which generally takes the form of play, either free or suggested; the sensorimotor and manipulative activities provided for the children (singing, drawing, rhythmics, etc.) help to awaken their personalities and to give them a sound emotional and mental balance.

21. Functional and individualized education, which is characteristic of the education of the young child, should not exclude group activities which contribute to character training, the education of the emotions and the development of the social sense.

22. At pre-primary level, it is important for intellectual education to be

based on the observation of the immediate surroundings and the development of oral expression, and, although all formal instruction must be excluded from this type of education, it is possible, from the age of five onwards and in so far as the child shows sufficient maturity and interest, to introduce him to the skills he will learn in school by means of graphic expression, the organization of concrete situations which can only be solved through the use of measure and number, and the utilization of specially designed materials.

23. Adequate time should be reserved for open-air activities and a proper balance should be achieved between free and directed activities.

24. With the reservation that the above-mentioned principles must be adhered to, teachers at pre-primary level should have wide freedom in their choice of procedure and in the preparation of their programme of activities, while being sure that they have at their disposal sufficiently varied material and all indispensable equipment.

25. As pre-primary education plays an important part in caring for the children's health, it should foster in them good health habits; furthermore, it is essential that school medical and child guidance services should be made available for them at least to the same extent as for primary school pupils.

26. Collaboration with the family is essential in pre-primary education; the aim of this collaboration is to make parents aware of their educational responsibilities and help them to assume them; it should not be limited simply to meeting parents who bring their child to school, but should comprise regular interviews, talks, discussion groups, if possible the parents' participation in certain school activities, occasional visits from them during class time, and also home visits by the teacher and, if need be, the social worker.

27. Wherever possible, psychological and educational research on pre-primary education should be undertaken more widely and more thoroughly; it is important that members of the teaching staff and parents should be kept informed of the practical results of such research by means of articles, lectures, talks on the radio, various publications, etc.

Teaching staff

28. As the education of children of pre-primary age presents psychological and educational problems of a particular kind, it is important that persons intending to take up this work should possess the necessary qualities and receive a specialized training which should be supplementary to a general training in education, and to this end it is desirable to create pilot institutions attached to teacher training establishments.

29. The studies and qualifications required of pre-primary teachers should be at least of the same standard as those required of primary teaching staff.

30. Where there is a shortage of qualified pre-primary teachers, it might be useful to organize emergency specialization courses for persons already possessing some educational experience and the necessary abilities, to be

followed later by in-service training which would gradually place them on the same level as qualified pre-primary teachers.

31. It is desirable to provide for teachers at pre-primary level, as for all other categories of teachers, opportunities for improving their efficiency and methods, whether by means of vacation, correspondence or other courses, or by lectures on education, periods of work in pilot institutions, etc.

32. Qualified pre-primary teachers should enjoy the same status (salary, working conditions, holidays, etc.) and the same advantages as primary teaching staff.

33. Equality as regards training, status and remuneration would help to facilitate the transfer of teachers from pre-primary to primary establishments, or vice versa; if necessary, suitable reorientation courses should be provided for the teachers concerned.

Building and equipment

34. All possible steps should be taken to ensure the children's safety; in towns, pre-primary education establishments should be situated near the parents' homes in order to reduce traffic dangers and avoid the use of transport.

35. All pre-primary education establishments should have their own buildings; they should possess a playground specially equipped to promote outdoor activities and also a garden, which, in addition to its aesthetic value, would permit the observation of nature, gardening and the rearing of small animals.

36. If premises intended for pre-primary education cannot form a separate building, they should be situated on the ground floor, in rooms which are sufficiently large and light, with an exit onto a playground reserved for children of pre-primary age and specially equipped for their use.

37. When the authorities issue licenses for the building of new housing estates, they should require, among other things, the provision of an adequate number of pre-primary education establishments, each having a playground which might remain at the children's disposal when the establishment is closed.

38. Particular care should be given to the decoration, furnishing and equipment of pre-primary education establishments; all these various elements should be adapted to the physical, educational and aesthetic needs of the children in accordance with their age; the younger the children the more free space should be placed at their disposal in each room.

39. As training in hygiene and cleanliness is an integral part of pre-primary education, it is important that special attention should be given to the provision of a supply of drinking water and that the sanitary installations should be adapted to the children's various ages and kept constantly in a state of perfect cleanliness and in good working order.

40. Pre-primary education establishments which fulfil a social purpose and in which the children remain all day must possess the necessary equipment for the preparation and distribution of meals and for the indispensable rest periods;

facilities should also be provided for temporarily isolating any child who may fall ill during the day.

International collaboration

41. It is desirable that countries which are contemplating the introduction of a system of pre-primary education should be able to call upon the help of experts from other countries with a view to the organization of pilot institutions and of courses for the training of specialized staff.

42. It would be useful for all countries, including those where pre-primary education already exists, to organize seminars and conferences at the international level for the examination of problems relating to young children and pre-primary education, and to facilitate the exchange of documents (official regulations, reports, specialized publications, films, children's books, educational materials, etc.) among teachers and specialists from the different countries; in this connection the cooperation of Unesco, the International Bureau of Education, the World Organization for Early Childhood Education, and other educational organizations and associations of a worldwide or regional nature might be called upon.

43. A scholarship system should assist specialists in pre-primary education to travel abroad or take courses in countries where this type of education is particularly well developed and especially where the economic, population and other conditions most resemble those of their own country.

Implementation

44. It is important that the text of this recommendation should be widely diffused by Ministries of Education, the school authorities for the level of education most directly concerned, national and international teachers' associations, etc.; the educational press, whether official or private, should play a large part in the diffusion of the recommendation.

45. Unesco regional centres, with the collaboration of the ministries concerned, are invited to facilitate the study of this recommendation at the regional level with a view to its adaptation to the special characteristics of the regions concerned.

46. In countries where it seems necessary, Ministries of Education are invited to request the competent bodies to undertake certain activities such as, for example:

(a) to examine the present recommendation and to compare it with the *de jure* and *de facto* situation in their respective countries;

(b) to consider the advantages and disadvantages of implementing each of the clauses not yet in force;

(c) to adapt each clause, should its implementation be considered useful, to the requirements of the individual country; and

(d) to suggest the regulations and practical measures which should be taken to ensure the implementation of each clause examined.

APPENDIX B

Council of Europe—Council for Cultural Co-operation
Venice Symposium—October 1971

Recommendations on Preschool Education

Recommendation A1

Whereas

1. Pre-school establishments do not exist solely for the purpose of looking after the children of working mothers, but should also provide the best possible conditions for the child's full physical, emotional, moral, social and intellectual development;

2. New emotional, intellectual and social needs arise around the age of three (depending on the child) which the family alone is scarcely able to satisfy;

3. The general development of the child depends on the number and nature of the stimuli he receives;

It is recommended

1. that governments realise the importance of pre-school education, both for the individual development of each child and for the general good of society; that all children, irrespective of social class, should by the age of three at latest be given the opportunity to attend a pre-school education establishment and that such establishments should therefore be set up and developed;

2. that the number of children per teacher at pre-primary level should be lower than the number of pupils in a primary school class and should be proportionately smaller as the children are younger, and never exceed twenty-five (based on Article 16 of Recommendation 53 of the International Conference on Public Education, Geneva, 1961).

Recommendation A2

In view of the need to develop pre-school education and considering that the child's development, however varied in its aspects and factors, is a single process and must be treated as such;

in order to avoid administrative confusion, overlapping, incoherency in the application of regulations and conflicts between various authorities;

in order to provide more children living in the same country with similar conditions of development;

It is recommended

1. that wherever local conditions allow, pre-school education be made subject to the authority of a single government department combining all teaching, administrative and social services;

2. that this department be the Ministry of Education;

3. that if all services cannot be combined in a single department, a co-ordinating service be set up to ensure that the administrative and pedagogical measures taken with regard to pre-school education are consistent;

4. that where there are pre-school establishments other than those organised by the State (whether completely private or supervised and subsidised by the State), legislative measures be taken to ensure that the conditions of accommodation and staff recruitment are such that the children attending them suffer no disadvantage by comparison with other children, and that the education they receive is of a sufficiently high standard;

5. that the curricular autonomy of pre-school education be recognised without its being allowed to become something separate from all other forms of education and that its autonomy be recognised by the creation of a special body of women inspectors of pre-school education;

6. that the liaison between pre-school and primary education be the more closely maintained, the greater the autonomy granted to the former (see Recommendation D1).

Recommendation A3

Having regard

1. to the importance of a rich, beautiful, varied and stimulating environment;

2. to the importance of adequate space;

3. to the need to compensate for the inadequacy of the family flat, the street or the neighbourhood in order to allow the child's personality to develop to the full;

4. to the risks to children from present-day traffic conditions;

It is recommended

1. that the construction of buildings and surroundings for pre-school establishments be supervised by a team consisting of architects, town planners, landscape artists, teachers, and representatives of parents' associations;

2. that the child's need for play-space and security be specifically taken into consideration by the authorities whenever new towns, districts or apartment

buildings are designed and built, and that play areas be reserved for the children;

3. that the pre-school establishments give the pupils training in self-protection against the dangers of road traffic in a manner suited to the age of each child.

Recommendation A4

Having regard to the present-day situation and the mobility of working people in Europe;

Having regard to the need for children to be assimilated as rapidly as possible by the society in which they will have to live and, more particularly, to acquire a language of communication;

Whereas it is recognised that each child, irrespective of the country in which his parents work, is entitled to the same opportunities for success at school and at work as all other children;

It is recommended that Member States:

1. urge migrant parents to send their children to a pre-school establishment as early as possible,

2. take measures to encourage migrants to learn the language of the host country.

Recommendation B1

Whereas,

1. the role of the family and that of the school are not strictly identical;

2. the action of the family and that of the school must be complementary;

3. the school must not be considered a substitute for the family;

And whereas,

1. the education given to the child must form a coherent whole;

2. present-day economic and social conditions do not always leave parents sufficient time to look after their children properly;

It is recommended

1. that the principle of the necessary relationship between school and family be applied in different ways and under different conditions according to local circumstances, and that appropriate measures be taken to organise the necessary co-operation between parents and teachers;

2. that pre-school establishments be given facilities to allow children to remain in them outside school hours, long enough to give parents the assurance that their children are safe when they themselves have sound reasons for being unable to look after them at home.

Recommendation B2

Having regard,

1. to the need to give the child proper education while he is still in the home environment;

2. to the need to establish co-operation between parents and teachers;

3. to the need to impart to parents a minimum of knowledge of the psychological development and needs of children and of the elementary rules of education;

It is recommended

1. that an elementary training programme for parents be introduced during the compulsory schooling period;

2. that modern communication media (press, radio, TV, etc.) be used to disseminate such information in a satisfactory manner, so as to add to the parents' knowledge in this field;

3. that parents be informed, by teachers and others, of the structure, objectives and methods of pre-school education;

4. that in the event of particularly acute conflicts between the school and the family, a team of specialists be called upon to overcome the difficulties as quickly and effectively as possible so that the children do not have to suffer the consequences.

Recommendation C1

Having regard,

1. to the importance of pre-school education in the child's later life;

2. to the number, variety and complexity of problems that arise in connection with the training of a young child, both psychologically and pedagogically;

3. to the need for the teacher and the child to remain in close contact with the world in which they live for the purpose of seizing educational opportunities and discovering applications for the knowledge acquired;

4. to the need for the child to be in contact with psychologically stable, balanced adults;

It is recommended

1. that pre-school teachers receive their training and specialisation at post-secondary level after having made a clear-cut choice;

2. that only candidates of sufficient maturity and psychological stability be selected for such training;

3. that the standard of education be the same as that demanded for primary school teachers;

4. that pre-school teachers be given the same professional status and pay as primary school teachers;

5. that a large proportion of their training be given over to the problems of the child's development in all its forms from birth to elementary school age, while not overlooking the other ages;

6. that teachers be given sufficient general training to enable them to understand fully their role in relation to the child and to society and to adapt themselves readily to the inevitable changes inherent in social evolution.

Recommendation C2

Having regard to the need (see Recommendations B1 and B2) to establish close contact between the home environment and the pre-school establishment and to enable the latter to play its part effectively in relation both to the children and to the parents;

It is recommended

1. that specific opportunities be found in training courses for future teachers to be made aware of the importance of the contribution of parents to the education of young children;

2. that future teachers be rendered capable of contributing to the training of parents (see Recommendation B2, para. 3 above);

3. that future teachers be informed of the existence of social welfare services and of the way they operate, so as to offer the parents help when needed (see Recommendation E);

4. that future teachers be initiated in the techniques of group discussion and leadership and the problems of group dynamics in order to improve their relations with parents.

Recommendation C3

Having regard to the need to establish a liaison between pre-school education and primary school education;

It is recommended

that during their training period, future primary school teachers receive part of their training in pre-school establishments and vice versa.

Recommendation C4

Having regard

1. to the present disintegration of family structures;

2. to the absence, often prolonged, of the father from the home;

It is recommended

that male teachers should not automatically be excluded from pre-school establishments.

Recommendation C5

Having regard

1. to the variety of staff required for the proper running of pre-school establishments;

2. to the need to set up coherent, efficient teams of teachers;

It is recommended

that the Council of Europe organise a symposium on matters of concern to all staff of pre-school establishments; their initial and in-service training, their recruitment and working conditions.

Recommendation D

Having regard

1. to the importance of preparing the pre-school child for the elementary school;

2. to the danger of early maladjustment to subsequent success at school;

3. to the psychological shocks that may be caused by a sudden change of environment, of teachers or of methods;

and in order to provide the vital link between pre-school education and primary education;

It is recommended

1. that all Member States ensure that children are prepared for this transition during the whole of their final year of pre-school education (by means of visits, meetings, etc.);

2. that systematic measures be taken to prepare parents for this transition by their children (changes in methods, in conditions of school life, etc.);

3. that the host environment (the primary school) for the first period of compulsory schooling be sufficiently flexible to adapt itself to the habits and needs of the children (particularly with regard to school hours and timetables);

4. that meetings between pre-school and primary teachers and inspectors be officially organised so that their mutual acquaintance may result in better comprehension and more effective co-operation;

5. that if a child shows signs of anxiety of any kind in or out of school, provision be made for special measures to be taken after talks between parents, teachers and, if need be, educational psychologists and doctors, for the purpose of early diagnosis;

6. that steps be taken to ensure that children who have been unable to attend a pre-school establishment can be introduced into a larger community than that of the family without running too great a risk.

Recommendation E

Whereas,

1. the psychology of the family environment affects the child's development;

2. the education of the child throughout the whole period between birth and the beginning of compulsory schooling can be provided in different environments (family, day-nursery, nursery school);

3. all educational action must endeavor to be coherent;

It is recommended

1. that social assistance measures be taken to ensure that all families can live in conditions of adequate security and that assistance may be rapidly provided by the proper services in case of need;

2. that all day-nurseries be considered not only as nurseries but as places of education designed to develop all aspects of the child's personality.

Recommendation F1

Having regard

1. to the number and magnitude of the problems discussed at the Venice Symposium;

2. to the real work done during the Symposium;

3. to the number of problems, and of aspects of problems, which could only be mentioned in passing and not studied in depth;

It is recommended

that the present members of the Symposium be given an opportunity to meet again in the future in order to make a more thorough study of the general problems left outstanding.

Recommendation F2

Having regard

1. to the number, variety and complexity of biological, psychological, social and pedagogical problems arising in connection with pre-school education;

2. to the need for teachers to be constantly provided with up-to-date information and to be informed of the latest results of scientific research;

3. to the need for pre-school education to be based on scientifically established findings and thereby to be constantly improved;

It is recommended

1. that action-research be organised in all countries;

2. that research be carried out in depth into certain specific subjects (development of language, for example);

3. that all research be of a multidisciplinary nature;

4. that the findings be centralised and disseminated by a special service set up in the Council of Europe;

5. that the Council of Europe undertake to publish an account of the educational and pedagogical situation in pre-school establishments in the various countries, indicating the trends which emerge, their causes, the experiments made and the methods adopted as a result.

Recommendation F3

Having regard

1. to the need for the present-day citizen to master a modern language other than his mother tongue;

2. to the results already obtained in certain countries though the early learning of a foreign language;

3. to the need to develop and control such action by giving it a firm scientific foundation;

It is recommended

that the Council of Europe organise a symposium on the problem of early bilingualism.

Recommendation F4

The working groups,

1. having considered the problems arising in connection with the early learning of reading, writing and mathematics at pre-school level;

2. having had insufficient time to deal fully with all problems connected with early learning;

Recommend

that a special meeting be organised to consider, in the light of present-day scientific findings, whether early training of this kind is advisable and feasible and, if so, in what conditions.

APPENDIX C

BASIC INFORMATION ON COUNTRIES STUDIED

Country	Population	Number of Children, Ages 0 to 4	Land Area
Hong Kong	3,948,179[1]	396,700[8]	403.7 sq mi
India	546,955,945[2]	78,688,100[9]	1,178,995 sq mi
Japan	108,430,000[3]	8,805,819[10]	142,726.5 sq mi
Korea, Republic of	31,460,000[4]	4,473,318[11]	38,452 sq mi
Malaysia	10,439,430[5]		
Peninsula of Malaysia	8,809,557	1,439,524[12]	50,806 sq mi
Sabah	653,604		29,388 sq mi
Sarawak	976,269		48,250 sq mi
Philippines	36,684,486[6]	6,527,367[13]	115,830 sq mi
Thailand	34,152,000[7]	4,239,315[14]	198,250 sq mi

Country	Gross National Product	Average Yearly Income	Percent Adult Literacy	National Language
Hong Kong	22,850[15]	444[22]	78.2[29]	Chinese and English
India	386.2[16]	88[23]	27.8[30]	Hindi
Japan	90,677[17]	2,462[24]	97.8[31]	Japanese
Korea, Republic of	3,875[18]	281[25]	68[32]	Korean
Malaysia	10,225[19]	391[26]	22.3[33]	Malay
Philippines	56.7[20]	254[27]	83[34]	Tagalog
Thailand	160.2[21]	193[28]	70.8[35]	Thai

NOTES

1 1971.
2 1971.
3 Aug. 1, 1973.
4 Oct. 1, 1970.
5 1970.
6 May 6, 1970.
7 April 1, 1970.
8 July 1, 1972, estimated.
9 April 1, 1971.
10 Oct. 1, 1970.
11 July 1, 1971, estimated.
12 July 1, 1970, estimated.
13 July 1, 1972, estimated.
14 April 25, 1960.
15 In thousand millions of dollars, Hong Kong, 1972.
16 In thousand millions of rupee, 1969.
17 In thousand millions of yen, 1972.
18 In thousand millions of won, 1972.
19 In thousand millions of Malaysian dollars, 1971.
20 In thousand millions of pesos, 1972.
21 In thousand millions of bahts, 1972.
22 In U.S. dollars, 1963.
23 In U.S. dollars, 1969.
24 In U.S. dollars, 1972.
25 In U.S. dollars, 1972.
26 In U.S. dollars, 1972.
27 In U.S. dollars, 1972.
28 In U.S. dollars, 1972.
29 In 1966, "adult" defined as 10+ years.
30 In 1961, 15+ years.
31 In 1960, 15+ years.
32 In 1966, 15+ years.
33 In 1960, 15+ years.
34 In 1970, 15+ years.
35 In 1960, 10+ years.

SOURCES

China, Republic of, Council for International Economic Cooperation and Development, *Taiwan Statistical Data Book 1973,* Executive Yuan, Taipei, 1973.

Paxton, John (ed.), *The Statesmen's Yearbook 1974–1975,* St. Martin's Press, New York, 1974.

United Nations, Statistical Office, Department of Economic and Social Affairs, *Demographic Yearbook 1971,* New York, United Nations, 1972.

_____, *Demographic Yearbook 1972,* New York, United Nations, 1973.

_____, *Statistical Yearbook 1973,* New York, United Nations, 1974.

United Nations Educational, Scientific and Cultural Organization, *Literacy 1969–1971: Progress Achieved in Literacy throughout the World,* Paris, 1972.

von der Mehden, Fred H., *Politics of the Developing Nations,* Prentice-Hall, Englewood Cliffs, N.J., 1964.

APPENDIX D

PARTICIPANTS AT THE BANGKOK CONFERENCE ON PRESCHOOL EDUCATION, December 3-5, 1969

Seela Chayaniyayodhin, Thailand
The College of Education
Bangkok

Norman K. Henderson, Hong Kong
Chairman and General Editor of the Hong Kong Council for Educational Research
Department of Education
University of Hong Kong

Frances Hon, Hong Kong
Head of the Kindergarten Section
Education Department of Hong Kong.

Kiyoko Kowashi, Japan
Kawamura Junior College
Tokyo

Shinichi Kuboniwa, Japan
Deputy Chief of Primary Education Section
Bureau of Primary and Secondary Education
Ministry of Education

Eun Wha Lee, Korea
Instructor
Department of Education
College of Education
Ewha Women's University

Puay Kheng Mah, Singapore
Supervisor of Preschool Education
Ministry of Education

Leela P. Manhas, India
Director of Early Childhood Education
Central Institute of Education
Delhi University Enclave

R. Muralidharan,   India
Reader
National Institute of Education
National Council of Educational
  Research and Training

Eiichi Okamoto,   Japan
National Institute of Educational
  Research

Hyun Ki Paik,   Korea
Director
Central Education Research Insti-
  tute

Lamaimas Saradatta,   Thailand
The College of Education
Bangkok

Miguela M. Solis,   Philippines
Director
National Coordinating Center for
  the Study and Development of
  Filipino Children and Youth

Ruth Wong,   Singapore
Director of Research
Ministry of Education

INDEX

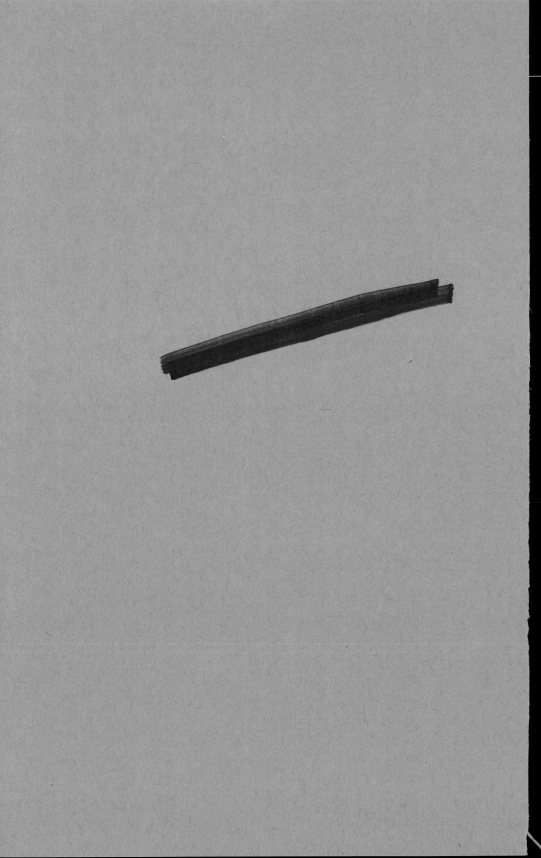